ICNC **MONOGRAPH** SERIES

Civil Resistance Tactics in the 21st Century

Michael A. Beer

Table of Contents

Summary 1

Introduction 3
    Why Study Civil Resistance Tactics? 5
    Main Findings of this Study 7
    Classifying Tactics: A Guiding Framework 8
    Monograph Overview 10

CHAPTER 1. **Basics of Civil Resistance** 11
    Defining Civil Resistance 11
    Mechanisms of Change 12
    Historical Examples 13
    Components of Civil Resistance 14
        • Tactics 14
        • Duration of a Tactic 15
        • Campaigns 16
        • Movements and Grand Strategy 17
    Universality and Context 18

CHAPTER 2. **Accounting for Tactical Innovation and Variety of Nonviolent Tactics** . . . 19
    Digital Technology: Growth and Documentation 19
    Arts-based and Cultural Resistance 21
    Human Rights Activism 23
    Diffusion of Knowledge About Civil Resistance 24
    Tactical Innovation from Women and Sexual/Gender Minorities 26
    Resistance to the Rise of Global Corporate Power 28
    Ongoing Repression 29
    Competition for Public Attention 29
    Competition for Resources among Groups within a Movement 30
    Natural or Human-induced Disasters 30

CHAPTER 3. Categorizing Nonviolent Tactics ... 32
Sharp's Classification of Nonviolent Methods ... 32
Disruptive and Constructive Resistance ... 34
Ebert's Categorization of Nonviolent Tactics ... 35
Mechanisms of Nonviolent Direct Action ... 37
Categorizing Based on Constructive/Persuasive and Confrontational/Coercive Inducements ... 38
Alternative Classifications of Nonviolent Tactics ... 41
- Civil Resistance Against Occupation ... 41
- Civil Defense ... 41
- Civil Resistance Against Corruption ... 42
- Everyday Resistance Against Structural and Institutional Dominance ... 43
- "Power-Breaking" Categorization ... 44

CHAPTER 4. Mapping New Civil Resistance Tactics ... 46

CHAPTER 5. New Civil Resistance Tactics: Selection Criteria, Descriptions, and Examples ... 50
The Criteria for Selecting New Civil Resistance Tactics ... 50
Tactics of "Saying" Something (Protest and Appeal) ... 51
- Human Body as the Primary Medium of Expression ... 51
- Material Art as the Primary Medium of Expression ... 52
- Digital/Internet Technology as the Primary Medium of Expression ... 53
- Human Language as the Primary Medium of Expression ... 54

Tactics of "Not Doing" (Noncooperation and Refraining) ... 55

Noncooperation Tactics: Confrontational Acts of Omission ... 56
- Political Noncooperation ... 56
- Social Noncooperation ... 56
- Economic Noncooperation ... 57

Refraining: Constructive Acts of Omission ... 57
- Suspending ... 58
- Active Abstention ... 58

Tactics of "Doing or Creating" Something (Disruptive and Creative Interventions) ... 59

Disruptive Intervention: Confrontational Acts of Commission ... 60
- Political/Judicial Disruptive Intervention ... 60
- Economic Disruptive Intervention ... 60
- Social Disruptive Intervention ... 61
- Physical Disruptive Intervention ... 61
- Psychological Disruptive Intervention ... 61

Creative Intervention: Constructive Acts of Commission ... 62
- Political/Judicial Creative Intervention ... 63
- Economic Creative Intervention ... 63
- Social Creative Intervention ... 64
- Physical Creative Intervention ... 65
- Psychological Creative Intervention ... 65

CHAPTER 6. **On the Edges of Civil Resistance Tactics** 66
    Everyday Resistance 66
    Property Destruction and Transformation 66
    Suicide 68
    Third-Party Nonviolent Actions 68
    Negotiation and Dialogue 69
    Lobbying 71
    Logistical Support Activities for Nonviolent Tactics 71
    Psychological Attack 72
    Actions Seemingly without a Strategic Goal 73

CHAPTER 7. **Key Takeaways** 74
    Takeaways for Activists 74
    Takeaways for Civil Resistance Scholars and Students 75
    Takeaways for Groups Interested in Supporting Nonviolent Movements 76

Cited Bibliography 78

Appendix: Universe of Nonviolent Tactics 83

Acknowledgements / About the Author 104

A Note from the Author 105

Tables and Figures

TABLE 1: **The Universe of Civil Resistance Tactics** 9

TABLE 2: **Components of Civil Resistance** 14

TABLE 3: **Ebert's Classification System (1970)** 36

TABLE 4: **Mapping New Civil Resistance Tactics** 48

FIGURE 1: **Constructive or Persuasive Tactics** 39

FIGURE 2: **Confrontational or Coercive Tactics** 39

SUMMARY

AS WITH WEAPONS OF VIOLENCE, the weapons of civil resistance are numerous, diverse, and ever-evolving. In addition to strikes, boycotts, mass demonstrations and other widespread actions, new tactics are regularly being invented as civil resisters adapt to opportunities, challenges, and tactics by their opponents.

The expanding repertoire of nonviolent tactics (sometimes referred to as methods by researchers like Gene Sharp) is a testament to the ingenuity and creativity of activists around the world. Exploring new tactics—the primary purpose of this monograph—is not just a simple documentation or classification exercise. Studying each individual method opens up a world of civil resistance stories in various places and times. Each method offers insight into people's perseverance and resilience in the face of repression, demonstrating not only a drive to fight for rights, freedom, and justice, but also the need to be innovative and adaptive in leading resistance struggles.

This monograph opens by introducing terms and fundamental concepts in civil resistance, followed by trends and underlying factors driving the growth of new civil resistance tactics worldwide. It then identifies shortcomings in the current categorization of tactics and offers an expanded list of new tactics as well as a refined framework for cataloging them. Finally, it offers clear takeaways for activists and practitioners, experts, researchers in the field, and others who are interested in supporting nonviolent movements effectively.

Introduction

NONVIOLENT CIVIL RESISTANCE OCCURS DAILY across many societies in a variety of forms. Examples include indigenous blockades against resource extraction in the Amazon, anti-corruption hunger strikes in Russia, street protests against dictators in the Middle East and North Africa, illegal same-sex wedding ceremonies in India, and whale protection by boat interventions in the Antarctic Ocean.

Coverage of civil resistance movements is increasingly available in many countries. Books[1] and films[2] recount the stories of nonviolent struggles and the ordinary people that led them. The *A Force More Powerful* documentary, which features historical civil resistance campaigns in India, South Africa, Chile, Denmark, the United States, and Poland, has reached

---

1 Some of the key generic books on civil resistance include (this list is not exhaustive or in a particular order): Erica Chenoweth and Maria Stephan, *How Civil Resistance Works* (New York: Columbia University Press, 2011); Peter Ackerman and Jack DuVall, *A Force More Powerful: A Century of Nonviolent Conflict* (New York: Macmillan, 2000); Maciej Bartkowski, ed., *Recovering Nonviolent History. Civil Resistance in Liberation Struggles* (Boulder CO: Lynne Rienner Publishers, 2013); Shaazka Beyerle, *Curtailing Corruption: People Power for Accountability and Justice* (Boulder CO: Lynne Rienner Publishers, 2014); Robert J. Burrowes, *The Strategy of Nonviolent Defense: A Gandhian Approach* (Albany: SUNY Press, 1996); Maia Carter Hallward and Norma M. Julie, *Understanding Nonviolence: Contours and Context* (Cambridge: Polity Press, 2015); Robert L. Helvey, *On Strategic Nonviolent Conflict: Thinking About the Fundamentals* (Boston: The Albert Einstein Institution, 2004); Sharon Erickson Nepstad, *Nonviolent Revolutions Civil Resistance in the Late 20th Century* (Oxford: Oxford University Press, 2011); Adam Roberts and Timothy Garton Ash, eds., *Civil Resistance and Power Politics: The Experience of Non-Violent Action from Gandhi to the Present* (Oxford: Oxford University Press, 2009); Kurt Schock, *Unarmed Insurrections: People Power Movements in Nondemocracies* (University of Minnesota Press, 2004); David Cortright, *Peace: A History of Movements and Ideas* (Cambridge University Press, 2008); Mary King, *Mahatma Gandhi and Martin Luther King, Jr.: The Power of Nonviolent Action* (UNESCO/Cultures of Peace, 1991); Maria J., Stephan, ed., *Civilian Jihad: Nonviolent Struggle, Democratization, and Governance in the Middle East* (New York: Palgrave Macmillian Series on Civil Resistance, 2010); Gene Sharp, *From Dictatorship to Democracy: A Conceptual Framework for Liberation*, Fourth Edition (Boston: Albert Einstein Institution, 2010); Gene Sharp, *The Politics of Nonviolent Action: Power and Struggle (Part One), The Methods of Nonviolent Action (Part Two), and The Dynamics of Nonviolent Action (Part Three)* (Boston: Porter Sargent Publishers, 1973).

2 Some of the documentaries on civil resistance struggles include: *Bringing Down a Dictator*; *Orange Revolution*; *Egypt: Revolution Interrupted?*; and *A Force More Powerful*, all of which are available to stream for free in numerous languages on ICNC's website, **https://www.nonviolent-conflict.org/icncfilms/**; and *Singing Revolution*; *Armenian Velvet Revolution*; among others.

tens of millions of viewers in numerous languages.[3] The Digital Library of Nonviolent Resistance[4] (which houses training manuals collected by Nonviolence International in partnership with the Rutgers International Institute for Peace), and the ICNC Online Resource Library (which offers civil resistance resources translated in many languages by the International Center on Nonviolent Conflict[5]) are just two of many websites that have made "how-to" and research information on civil resistance available on a global scale.

However, despite widespread interest in the subject, the most comprehensive effort to catalog the wide array of nonviolent tactics is still Gene Sharp's 198 nonviolent methods, an extensive list complete with descriptions, examples, and categories that was published in 1973. Since then, there has not been a comprehensive effort to significantly update this acclaimed list. Nonviolent tactics or methods[6] can be thought of as nonviolent weapons or tools that are typically utilized as alternatives to violent (or armed) resistance. As with weapons of violence, the weapons of nonviolent conflict are numerous, diverse, and ever-evolving. A few notable examples include boycotts, strikes, teach-ins, parallel governments, blockades, and marches.

Since 2016, Nonviolence International (NI)[7] has been collecting and identifying new methods of civil resistance in the Nonviolent Tactics Database.[8] This monograph emerged out of this cataloging process and answers three questions:

1. What tactics did Sharp not identify and what new tactics of civil resistance have emerged since 1973?

---

3   The *A Force More Powerful* documentary is available at: **https://www.nonviolent-conflict.org/force-powerful-english/**.

4   The Digital Library of Nonviolent Resistance is available at: **http://nonviolence.rutgers.edu/s/digital**.

5   The International Center on Nonviolent Conflict (ICNC) was founded in 2002 by Peter Ackerman and Jack DuVall and is a private operating foundation focused on how ordinary people nonviolently struggle and achieve rights, justice, and freedom worldwide: **https://www.nonviolent-conflict.org/**.

6   In this monograph, the term "tactics" will be used interchangeably with the term "methods." Tactics will be defined in detail on page 17. Though broader in its meaning, the term "nonviolent actions," unless indicated in the text otherwise, is also oftentimes used synonymously with "nonviolent tactics."

7   Nonviolence International (NI) was founded in 1989 by Mubarak Awad to continue his efforts to promote nonviolent action around the world after being expelled from Palestine by the Israeli government. NI is a network of resource centers that researches and promotes nonviolent action and a culture of peace and seeks to reduce violence and passivity worldwide. **http://nonviolentaction.net/**.

8   The Nonviolent Methods Database was created in 2016 by NI to expand the documentation of methods worldwide. It documents more than 300 methods, with descriptions and examples. The data are available for universal use on **https://www.tactics.nonviolenceinternational.net/**, and can be made available for use on other websites. Corrections and additions are welcome at **info@nonviolenceinternational.net**.

2. What new categorization of tactics can be helpful in documenting and understanding this common human activity?

3. How can this new knowledge—on tactics and classification—be helpful to practitioners and scholars of civil resistance, as well as those who would like to assist nonviolent movements?

This new effort also builds on the work of others. Groups including New Tactics in Human Rights, Beautiful Trouble, Gadjah Mada University's database of nonviolent methods,[9] Şiddetsizlik Eğitim ve Araştırma Dernegi,[10] the Global Nonviolent Action Database,[11] and the Meta-Activism Project[12] are also collecting and cataloguing tactics and examples, many of which are now collated into the Nonviolent Tactics Database and introduced in this monograph.[13]

Why Study Civil Resistance Tactics?

Studying tactics may inspire and promote action, deepen scholarly understanding, help recover nonviolent history, improve skills through education and training, and improve strategic planning.

To Inspire and Promote Action

Sharp's list of 198 methods (1973) has been translated into many languages and has inspired countless activists and educators. Unfortunately, the list is over 45 years old and the described methods were deployed in historical contexts that are sometimes unknown or far removed from contemporary activists and analysts.

Often the biggest barriers to action are despair, ignorance, and fear. These human emotions discourage or blind activists from seeing the wide range of possible nonviolent methods at their disposal. Worse, these emotions sometimes push activists to consider engaging in counter-productive violence. Thus, studying hundreds of nonviolent tactics and examples of

---

9   The Department of International Relations at Universitas Gadjah Mada maintains an ongoing database of more than 6,000 events of Indonesian nonviolent actions and methods. This is not yet publicly available.

10 The Nonviolent Education and Research Center in Istanbul, set up by NI in 2012, has a dataset of nonviolent actions in the Turkish language.

11 The Global Nonviolent Action Database can be accessed at: **https://nvdatabase.swarthmore.edu/**.

12 The Meta-Activism Project analyzes the field of digital activism. It is available at: **www.meta-activism.org**.

13 An additional resource is the website Actipedia, which describes itself as an "open-access, community-generated wiki to document, share, and inspire activists to conduct creative action." The site serves as an archive of tactics. The website does not currently organize the featured actions into categories that could be useful for comparative analysis. **https://actipedia.org/**.

their deployment helps to convey the enormous range of actions that are available to humanity, regardless of the political systems they live under.

To Deepen Scholarly Understanding

The study of tactics is a basic foundation for understanding and researching the nature, dynamics, and effects of nonviolent struggle. Ronald McCarthy in Protest, Power, and Change (1997, 320) argues that tactics of nonviolent action: (1) are based on observable phenomena, independent of views of nonviolent resistance that might vary according to time and locality, and (2) provide an indicator for the occurrence of nonviolent action in conflicts that, in turn, allows verifiable and replicable research findings to be made. Identifying and cataloguing new civil resistance tactics in new contexts—a primary undertaking of this monograph—therefore enriches our understanding of how the creative agency of ordinary people drives nonviolent resistance and change.

To Recover the History of Nonviolent Resistance

Violent methods have had a powerful impact on historical change, yet modern life has been strongly influenced by other forms of collective action, including methods of nonviolent resistance and defiance. Maciej Bartkowski (2013) is one of many researchers who have used knowledge of nonviolent tactics to excavate history and uncover protests, strikes, and other nonviolent actions in many societies under colonialism and foreign occupation. Nonviolence International's book on Tibetan nonviolent tactics and struggle, entitled Truth is Our Only Weapon (2000), changed many Tibetans' understanding of their own history of resistance. The book quickly became a standard textbook in schools for Tibetan exiles.[14] Other scholarly works on nonviolent action have changed the foundational myths for the British, American, Russian, and Cuban revolutions that previously centered on armed revolt or legislative enactments.[15] Updating the repository of nonviolent tactics provides us with additional markers to highlight the use of civil resistance throughout history and across different geographies and cultures.

---

14   Fourteen years later, in 2014, the International Center on Nonviolent Conflict published a monograph by a Tibetan diaspora activist Tenzin Dorjee that offered a comprehensive historical analysis of the Tibetan uprisings and resistance, starting from the 1950s until the last revolution of 2008 and its aftermath. See *The Tibetan Nonviolent Struggle: A Strategic and Historical Analysis*, ICNC Monograph Series, 2014: **https://www.nonviolent-conflict.org/the-tibetan-nonviolent-struggle-a-strategic-and-historical-analysis-2/**.

15   These scholarly works include: Ackerman, Peter, and Christopher Kruegler. *Strategic Nonviolent Conflict: The Dynamics of People Power in the Twentieth Century*. Westport, CT: Praeger, 1994; Bartkowski, Maciej J. *Recovering Nonviolent History: Civil Resistance in Liberation Struggles*. Boulder, CO: Lynne Rienner Publishers, 2013; McManus, Philip, and Gerald Schlabach. *Relentless Persistence: Nonviolent Action in Latin America*. Eugene, Or.: Wipf & Stock, 2004; Schell, Jonathan. *The Unfinished Twentieth Century: The Crisis of Weapons of Mass Destruction*. London: Verso, 2003.

To Educate and Train

Beyond studying nonviolent tactics, one may also train to use them. Studying tactics is helpful for planning, but training is usually necessary for successful action. In a 2016 study on training for civil resistance campaigns, Nadine Bloch notes that tactics are commonly shared in the form of training manuals, classes, and how-to videos. Bloch points out that training programs improve unity, discipline, and successful attainment of goals (2016, 14).

In order to be successful, nonviolent actions, such as a strike, a banner-hang, or a tree sit against logging, require skill development. Using a tactic in a particular context often requires many constituent components, including planning, organizing and logistics, and training. In case of a possible arrest or risk of injury, additional actions must be undertaken, such as medical care, legal assistance, jail support and solidarity, bail money, documentation, and long-term psycho-social support.

To Improve Strategic Planning

Without efforts to analyze nonviolent tactics, one cannot discern or devise a strategy for an effective campaign. The strategy that takes into consideration, among others, timing, duration, choice of tactics, required resources, and their sequence of deployment is particularly significant in the battle that the Nobel Laureate, Thomas Schelling (1968), compared to bargaining:

> *The tyrant and his subjects are in somewhat symmetrical positions. They can deny him most of what he wants—they can, that is, if they have the disciplined organization to refuse collaboration. And he can deny them just about everything they want—he can deny it by using the force at his command... It is a bargaining situation in which either side, if adequately disciplined and organized, can deny most of what the other wants; and it remains to see who wins.*

Many nonviolent actions can fail because there is little tactical understanding of how to prepare for, perform, and reap strategic benefits from them. In some cases, activists under- or over-estimate the resources and organizing required, or fail to accurately calculate the costs and risks associated with an action. Identifying which tactics will be most successful in a conflict provides campaigners with opportunities to effectively deploy them as well as identify and assess their desired outcomes.

Main Findings of this Study

There are more methods of nonviolent civil resistance beyond the 198 methods previously documented by Sharp and other scholars. Our current Nonviolent Tactics Database includes more than 346 methods (see Universe of Nonviolent Tactics Appendix). Sharp was the first to admit that his compilation of methods was incomplete.[16] New civil resistance tactics are regularly being invented or recognized precisely because civil resistance is a widespread, continuous occurrence in a multitude of societies and contexts, perpetually reinventing itself to accommodate for shifting conditions or to utilize new technologies of the day. Taking this into account, this monograph seeks to build on the enormous contribution that Sharp's work has made to the study of civil resistance worldwide.

Digital tactics of civil resistance are numerous, diverse, and widespread. The most striking new development since Sharp's book was published is the invention and growth of digital communication, primarily through the Internet. The Internet includes the worldwide web, mobile phones, email, apps, cloud computing, lasers, drones, robots, and "the Internet of things," such as household appliances, vehicles, and medical devices. Cyber actions, such as the creation of online petitions, Twitter bombs, and social media profile photos, are primarily acts of expression as defined and categorized in this monograph (see Table 1 below). The emergence of online communities and cyber-based work has birthed many new tactics of noncooperation, active disobedience, and constructive action, such as doxing (publicizing someone's personal information) and crowd-sourcing apps. Modern electronic media amplifies nonviolent actions to wide audiences, thus impacting tactics and messaging.

Classifying Tactics: A Guiding Framework

This monograph argues that the universe of civil resistance tactics can be usefully organized into three general categories:

- Saying (acts of expression)
- Not doing (acts of omission)
- Doing and creating (acts of commission)

each of which can be enacted in:

- Confrontational (coercive) or
- Constructive (persuasive) ways.

The table below illustrates the guiding framework this monograph uses to classify the universe of civil resistance tactics.

---

16   The Nonviolent Tactics Database is available at: **https://tactics.nonviolenceinternational.net**.

TABLE 1: The Universe of Civil Resistance Tactics

Resistance behavior	NATURE OF TACTIC INDUCEMENTS	
	CONFRONTATIONAL (COERCIVE)	**CONSTRUCTIVE (PERSUASIVE)**
Saying (acts of expression)[17]	**Protest** Communicative actions to criticize or coerce (example: a march)	**Appeal** Communicative actions to reward or persuade (example: a teach-in)
Not doing (acts of omission)[18]	**Noncooperation** Refusal to engage in expected behavior (examples: strikes and boycotts)	**Refraining** Halting or calling off a planned or ongoing action to reward or persuade (example: suspending a strike)
Doing or creating (acts of commission)[19]	**Disruptive intervention** Direct action that confronts another party to stop, disrupt, or change their behavior (example: a blockade)	**Creative intervention** Direct action that models or constructs alternative behaviors and institutions or takes over existing institutions (examples: a parallel government or kiss-in)

Table 1 introduces the concepts and categories of nonviolent tactics, which are the weapons or tools of nonviolent action and vary widely depending on their use in different conflicts. The categorization of tactics is based on broad behavioral resistance domains of saying, doing, and not doing.[20] Tactics are further categorized by the nature of their inducement as either coercive or persuasive. There is a dashed line between protest and appeal actions to signify that many acts of expression can be used for both constructive and confrontational purposes. Some expressive tactics like pray-ins are overwhelmingly on the appeal side. Other expressive tactics like rude gestures are overwhelmingly on the protest side. Yet others such as a speech of defiance can be used to appeal as well as to protest.

It also must be noted that disruptive interventions clearly involve coercive/confrontational inducements, whereas creative interventions are more complex. Even though the latter are clearly associated with the constructive/persuasive side, they might sometimes also operate coercively. For the purpose of this study, this monograph adopts an ideal analytical division with creative interventions assigned only to the constructive/persuasive inducements.

---

17   Saying (expression) is identical to Sharp's protest and persuasion (1973).

18   Sharp fully developed the understanding of the category of noncooperation.

19   Burrowes (1996) may have been the first to divide Sharp's intervention category into disruptive and creative intervention and to introduce a useful strategic distinction between tactics of concentration (coming together to engage in a specific action) and dispersion (spreading out across different locations to engage in a specific action).

20   These behavioral domains match precisely Sharp's categories of protest and persuasion, noncooperation, and intervention.

Monograph Overview

This monograph begins with an introduction to conflict, nonviolent action, and the components of civil resistance, including the importance of tactics. It then highlights general trends driving the innovation of new civil resistance tactics and discusses the underlying factors that account for that growth.

The study then reviews relevant literature on civil resistance tactics to identify significant contributions on the subject and point out the existing gaps and shortcomings in the current categorization of tactics. It also clarifies the need to compile and examine the new types of tactics that activists have invented and deployed over the past few decades.

The monograph then lays out the criteria for selecting new civil resistance methods and introduces a refined categorization for their cataloging. It presents and elaborates on a sampling of new methods, as identified in Table 1 and Table 4. It also discusses a variety of resistance tactics whose inclusion in civil resistance campaigns and nonviolent movement scholarship and education are controversial.

Lastly, the monograph offers insights into how the understanding of these new tactics and their classification can be helpful for activists and practitioners, experts, researchers in the field, and others who are interested in supporting nonviolent movements effectively.

CHAPTER 1. Basics of Civil Resistance

Large-scale political conflict can occur within routine and regulated resolution procedures such as elections, parliaments, and courts. Conflicts can also be conducted through mass direct action in violently disruptive (e.g., guerrilla war) or nonviolently contentious ways (e.g., strikes or demonstrations). Most conflicts are power struggles. Both violent and nonviolent struggles employ social, economic, political, psychological, and physical pressures and incentives to obtain their goals. In contrast to armed or violent resistance, nonviolent tactics are the key building blocks to civil resistance.

Defining Civil Resistance

Close to 100 years ago, Gandhi adopted the English term "civil resistance" as he felt that it most appropriately and comprehensively described the Indian independence struggle against British colonization.[21] In the decades that followed, several scholars have offered various definitions of civil resistance. This monograph will adopt the definition that Véronique Dudouet provided in her special report, *Powering to Peace: Integrated Civil Resistance and Peacebuilding Strategies* (2017, 5):

> *Civil resistance is an extra-institutional conflict-waging strategy in which organized grassroots movements use various [...] nonviolent tactics such as strikes, boycotts, demonstrations, noncooperation, self-organizing, and constructive resistance to fight perceived injustice without the threat or use of violence.*

This definition helps us view nonviolent tactics broadly. For example, a specific tactic such as civil disobedience is too often understood as equivalent to civil resistance. This single tactic of breaking laws that are perceived as unjust to achieve a political goal is only a tiny part of the larger civil resistance phenomenon. Many other nonviolent tactics are disruptive but not necessarily illegal such as boycotts, street theater, and hunger strikes. Strikes that may be routine in some countries are considered illegal in others. Context matters, and our definition of civil resistance tries to capture this by emphasizing the extra-institutional nature of actions. Civil resistance has been called by several other names in different contexts, including people power, nonviolent struggle, nonviolent mass action, nonviolent conflict, and political defiance.

---

21 In his 1935 letter "Servants of Indian Society," Gandhi wrote: "The statement that I had derived my idea of civil disobedience from the writings of Thoreau is wrong. The resistance to authority in South Africa was well advanced before I got the essay of Thoreau on civil disobedience. But the movement was then known as passive resistance. As it was incomplete, I had coined the word satyagraha for the Gujarati readers. When I saw the title of Thoreau's great essay, I began the use of his phrase to explain our struggle to the English readers. But I found that even civil disobedience failed to convey the full meaning of the struggle. I therefore adopted the phrase civil resistance." See Peter Ackerman, "Strategic Nonviolence is not Civil Resistance," *Minds of the Movement*, International Center on Nonviolent Conflict, September 21, 2017.

The power of civil resistance derives from the simple fact that rulers cannot sustain their rule and may fall when their soldiers, civil servants, or general population refuse to obey. Physical and coercive repression to stop civil resistance are typical responses from movement opponents. Yet research shows that compared to repression against armed or violent resistance, repression against civil resistance often backfires against the government,[22] and helps strengthen the movement by triggering loyalty shifts and even defections among key sectors of society such as the civil service, police, or military, which further limits the government's power.[23] Withdrawing cooperation and consent and eliciting defections from regime supporters without violence are hallmarks of civil resistance.

Violent collective action and actions as part of routinized politics within established institutions (such as legislative processes, government regulations, courts, and elections), are not considered tactics of civil resistance, even if they are sometimes intertwined or concurrent with nonviolent campaigns (Bond, et. al. 1997).[24]

Mechanisms of Change

George Lakey (1963) was the first to identify the range of successful outcomes of civil resistance campaigns against a movement opponent. Sharp (1973) later elaborated upon this work. The range of success outcomes includes conversion, accommodation, coercion, and disintegration of a movement opponent.[25] Withdrawal is potentially a fifth opponent response to a campaign.

---

[22] Brian Martin's research on backfire documents the frequent political loss of legitimacy and public support when violent repression is used to suppress nonviolent opposition. See **https://www.bmartin.cc/pubs/backfire.html**.

[23] For more information on defections, see: Binnendijk, Anika Locke. "Holding Fire: Security Force Allegiance during Nonviolent Uprisings," 2009; Binnendijk, Anika Locke, and Ivan Marovic. "Power and Persuasion: Nonviolent Strategies to Influence State Security Forces in Serbia (2000) and Ukraine (2004)." *Communist and Post-Communist Studies* 39, no. 3 (2006): 411–29; Nepstad, Sharon Erickson. *Nonviolent Revolutions: Civil Resistance in the Late 20th Century*. Oxford: Oxford University Press, 2011.

[24] Bond, Jenkins, Taylor, and Schock (1997, 556-559) developed a comprehensive framework for differentiating between nonviolent civil resistance, violent mass action, and legislative/routinized action. The framework is based on three dimensions: contentiousness (non-routine versus routine action), coerciveness (strong to weak inducements), and the outputs and outcomes (violent to nonviolent). Contentious actions can range from routine governmental lawmaking to disruptive illegal occupations and terrorist attacks. Some nonviolent action becomes so routine and predictable (getting arrested for sitting down in front of a government building) that these actions can be considered institutional/regulated actions. Coercive action refers to the negative and positive sanctions or inducements made on an opponent, often measured by the strength or intensity of the action. Coercive actions can include anything from fines and killing at the hands of rulers, to armed theft and blockades. Violent/nonviolent outcomes are the third distinction, which generally refers to damage to persons or property (or not).

[25] Bond further explains the four mechanisms in his chapter, "Nonviolent Direct Action and the Diffusion of Power," in *Justice Without Violence* by Wehr, Burgess, Burgess, eds. (Lynne Rienner Publishers, 1994, 70-74).

- Conversion is when a movement opponent fully accepts movement goals and rationale.

- Accommodation is the partial acceptance of movement demands based on the movement opponent's cost/benefit analysis.

- Coercion is surrendering to movement demands when sufficient pillars of support for the movement opponent have been removed because of loyalty shifts and defections.

- Disintegration happens when the public aligns its support with a new government and support for the old government collapses.

- Withdrawal occurs when an opponent moves away and at least temporarily cedes the field to a movement challenger.

Accommodation, coercion, and disintegration are the results of different degrees of power shifts within a society. Civil resistance is based on the fundamental insight that Sharp (1979) articulates as follows: "All governments depend on the sources of power which come from the society, and are made available because of the assistance, cooperation, and obedience of members of that society." While seeking to persuade the opponent, if possible, civil resistance is primarily focused on wielding popular power to withdraw and restrict social assistance, cooperation, and obedience from key sectors of society.

Historical Examples

Some successful examples of civil resistance to defeat dictators include the Solidarity movement (*Solidarność*) in Poland (1980s), the nationalist movements in the Soviet Union (1990s), the anti-Apartheid movement in South Africa (1980s), and the Islamic Revolution in Iran (1979) (for more, see Ackerman and DuVall, 2000; the Global Nonviolent Action Database; ICNC Conflict Summaries[26]). Examples of partially successful global nonviolent movements for human rights and liberation in the last 200 years include women's rights, lesbian, gay, bisexual, transgender, and queer (LGBTQ) rights, workers' rights, rights for people with disabilities, indigenous rights, and a great range of environmental causes. Examples of nonviolent campaign failures include the uprising at Tiananmen Square, China (1989), the environmental and minority rights campaign by Ken Saro Wiwa in the Niger Delta (1995), and Zimbabwe's democracy movement (2010s).

---

26 ICNC Conflict Summaries are available at: **https://www.nonviolent-conflict.org/nonviolent-conflict-summaries/**.

These examples of civil resistance or, as Schell calls it, nonviolent cooperative power (2001) demonstrate the fragility of rulers or majority cultures when they do not have strong support or consent from their society.

Components of Civil Resistance

Civil resistance is complex. It usually involves many people and institutions with varying needs, interests, inter-dependencies, and values interacting in complicated societies. One way to deconstruct civil resistance into understandable parts is to break it into stages of conflict, such as Ebert's three stages (for more on Ebert's classification, see Table 3).[27] Another way to understand civil resistance (as well as violent resistance) is to look at its common components. These components are described in Table 2, which divides civil resistance into three levels: actions, campaigns, and movements. It shows the relationship between tactics and other common elements within civil resistance. This, in turn, allows us to differentiate a tactic from other components of civil resistance and define it in more precise terms. The three levels of civil resistance also serve as a useful guide for targeting training and education to various audiences.

TABLE 2: Components of Civil Resistance

LEVELS OF RESISTANCE	PURPOSE/ENDS	MEANS	TYPICAL DURATION
Action	Limited (tactical) objectives	Tactic	Hours and days (much variation)
Campaign	Goal(s)	Strategy	Months and years
Movement	Vision(s)	Grand strategy	Years and decades

Tactics

Nonviolent action, as opposed to passivity, routine activity, and institutional procedures, is the basis of civil resistance. Tactics or methods are akin to nonviolent "weapons" and are "the many individual forms of action" (Sharp 2005, 445). Tactics can be best understood as

---

27 There are many models on how civil resistance develops over time. One group of models emerges from the perspective of civil resistance practitioners including: Bill Moyer's eight stages for social movements; George Lakey's five components of a nonviolent revolution; the six stages of Kingian nonviolence; and Gandhi's four stages: first, they ignore you, then they laugh at you, then they fight you, then you win. A second group of civil resistance stages is outlined by conflict managers and peacebuilders who look at conflict from "above" and see variations of stages such as latent, overt, settlement, perceived, felt, manifest, and aftermath in conflict. See for example Curle (1971).

discrete methods deployed to achieve a limited goal. A hunger strike in prison to demand better food and visiting privileges is a tactic because it is a specific action and has an objective. From 1993 to 1996, in Jakarta, Indonesia, East Timorese students seeking self-determination—for which there was no plausible legal recourse—climbed over fences onto the grounds of the U.S., Swedish, Finnish, Russian, and other embassies, all of which were territories immune from Indonesian arrest without embassy approval. Their tactical objective was to use serial and sustained occupations to make visible, and gain support for, their demands for self-determination to Indonesian and global audiences.

Civil resistance practitioners typically use the term "tactics" instead of "methods." "Tactics" is also the standard term used to describe forms of action on a limited scale by most social and political scientists. Although the distinction between "method" and "tactic" can be useful for research and educational purposes, the use of the word "methods" in many contexts is an obstacle to public understanding of civil resistance because of its general, ambivalent meaning. In many contexts, the term "nonviolent tactics" substitutes entirely for "methods" and, in other situations, as it will be the case in this monograph, methods and tactics are used interchangeably.

Duration of a Tactic

The duration of a tactic depends on the objective and therefore varies according to context. Implementing a tactic such as a march or a die-in takes time, resources, and effort—and often risk. Typically, many methods of expression and intervention (flash-mob, parade, etc.) are short-lived and last from minutes to days. Different movement actors therefore deploy methods for short durations and serially or progressively. Tactics such as Palestinians raising their flag in occupied territories during the 1980s had various durations and were implemented serially, perhaps thousands of times. One limited objective of this tactic was to break an unjust law banning display of the Palestinian flag. Another objective was to pressure Israel to use armed actors and resources to respond to the symbolic protests and to exhaust their resources and collective will to enforce the prohibition.

Tactics of omission such as boycotts and strikes are sometimes more sustainable and can last for an extended period of time. In the 18th century, residents of American colonies withheld taxes from the British for five months. When the British repealed the tax, the tax withholding campaign ended. Many other tax withholding efforts have lasted years.

Most nonviolent tactics are deployed in the context of campaigns, but some tactics are deployed with no campaign goals and without a campaign strategy. Uncoordinated tactics are also used by movement allies who are motivated to do something on their own regardless of other strategically planned movement actions.

To be implemented effectively, some methods might require years of study and training. For example, entire books have been published on boycotts, civil disobedience, strikes, and fasting.[28] Other methods require specialized skills such as sky-writing, or rope-climbing for banner hangs.

Campaigns

Civil resistance campaigns use nonviolent tactics and organizing to achieve a specific and long-lasting political or social change goal. Campaigns commonly last six months to two years. The Salt Satyagraha (1930-31) in India was a campaign consisting of a salt march to the town of Dandi on the Arabian Sea coast that began on March 12, 1930, as well as several subsequent marches and attempts to occupy salt works. In parallel, the campaign called for nationwide civil disobedience and boycotting of British goods. This lasted almost a year and ended when Gandhi negotiated with Lord Irwin, the British Viceroy of India, a truce that led to the formalized pact signed between the two on March 5, 1931. Gandhi's campaign attained two advances: the salt tax was revoked in response to the act of mass civil disobedience near the sea coast, and the British were forced to negotiate in a way that legitimized the equality of Indians.

Some tactics of nonviolent resistance are so impactful that they are strongly identified with a particular campaign. "Defining methods" (Schock, 2012) are used as the central technique around which campaigns are organized. For example, according to Beyerle (2014), Koreans identified political corruption as the largest hinderance for the betterment of the country. Civil society organizations, with the support of the public, created a blacklist of corrupt candidates considered unfit to run for parliamentary seats and designed a nonviolent campaign around it in order to oust corrupt officials from government. In Brazil, landless peasants used occupation as the primary method to meet their needs for subsistence and to campaign for more equal access to natural resources.

The use of one or many nonviolent tactics alone is usually not sufficient for waging a successful nonviolent campaign. A strategy is needed, reflected, among others, in:

- Sustained, multitudinous participation (Chenoweth and Stephan, 2011)
- Resilience in the face of repression (Sharp, 1973)
- Effective targeting of the opponents' support networks (Schock, 2005)

---

28   For more information, see: Awad, Mubarak, and Laura Bain. *Fasting: Pamphlet No.3 in a Series on Organizing Tactics for Nonviolent Action*. Nonviolence International, 2014; Herngren, Per. *Path of Resistance: the Practice of Civil Disobedience*. Philadelphia, PA: New Society Publishers, 1993; Feldman, David. *Boycotts Past and Present: from the American Revolution to the Campaign to Boycott Israel*. Cham, Switzerland: Palgrave Macmillan, 2019; Reichard, Richard W. *From the Petition to the Strike: a History of Strikes in Germany, 1869 - 1914*. New York: Peter Lang Inc., International Academic Publishers, 1991.

- Adherence to 12 strategic principles (Ackerman and Kruegler, 1994), later reduced to six key factors that make movements effective (Ackerman and Merriman, 2015), including unity, strategic planning, nonviolent discipline, participation growth, managing repression, and facilitating defections from opponents' allies in favor of a movement

A valuable source of information about strategically driven campaigns is the Global Nonviolent Action Database, which is based at Swarthmore College and has documented more than 1,400 nonviolent campaigns in various areas of human activity. It systematically registers the major actors, issues, strategies, and methods used in each campaign as well as the responses of the campaign's adversaries. It is an invaluable resource for activists, teachers, and researchers.

Movements and Grand Strategy

A civil resistance movement is a collection of campaigns that aim to implement a similar vision for society. Most movements can take years to achieve substantial success. A few are fairly centrally managed. Others can be geographically spread-out with autonomous local groups adhering to the general goals and directives set by the movement thought leaders. Some examples include the Burmese democracy movement (1990s), the East Timorese independence movement, and the Solidarity movement in Poland. Others are more loosely coordinated, such as the South African anti-Apartheid struggle, the current global movement for environmental justice, and various Arab Spring movements (2010s).

Grand strategy is needed to coordinate campaigns, or at least establish policies that seek to maximize mutual support and minimize internal conflict. For example, suffrage movements in various countries often split between suffragettes who carried out confrontational (coercive) tactics and those who employed constructive (persuasive) tactics and legal methods. Differing visions within movements also create conflict. In Burma in the 1990s, Burmans (the majority ethnic group) wanted an end to military rule because they wanted democracy, while the ethnic minorities wanted an end to military rule because they wanted autonomy and decentralized ethnic rule.

Grand strategy in movements serves as a constant reference—a guiding star. This is particularly helpful during times of rapid growth in movement participation, or when internal conflict arises. Movements can refer to their grand strategy for insight into which strategies and tactics to use, where their priorities should lie, and how to coordinate sequencing of campaign actions. Sometimes adopting a grand strategy helps activists mitigate disagreements over vision, especially when movement support is low or during repression.

Civil resistance movements frequently co-exist with external allies, and sometimes even with autonomous armed elements. In such circumstances, nonviolent movements must develop a viable grand strategy in order to successfully coordinate their strategies, negotiate and compromise with allies, and advance or defend their nonviolent stance.

In the 1990s, nonviolent resistance to the military regime was active in the heartland of Burma through the National League for Democracy, led by Aung San Suu Kyi. Simultaneously, on the perimeter of the country, ethnic minorities primarily engaged in armed resistance against the regime through the National Democratic Front. Internationally, the exile government was called the National Coalition Government of the Union of Burma. Finally, the National Council of the Union of Burma served as an over-arching coordination group for these various opposition groups. The grand strategy of the Burmese opposition required geographic, demographic, and organizational separation to avoid contamination of the nonviolent campaigns as well as to maintain coordination among various opposition groups to maximize synchronicity and cooperation.

Universality and Context

Civil resistance occurs in all societies but is an observable phenomenon that varies greatly according to context. For example, the use of civil disobedience varies widely depending on the laws or established norms it challenges. Chewing gum in Singapore, swimming with individuals of different ethnicities in apartheid South Africa, eating in public during the daytime fast of Ramadan in Morocco, or speaking Kurdish in Turkey are all actions that could be considered routine and insignificant elsewhere but are acts of civil disobedience in the specified contexts. However, regardless of the contexts of time, culture, belief system, and location, there are common patterns of defiant methods of action employed to induce a change in opponents' behavior. Just as atoms and quarks are essential to understanding the physical universe, nonviolent tactics are essential to understanding civil resistance and many modern conflicts.

Now that we have explored a number of broad notions about civil resistance, we can examine nonviolent tactics more deeply.

CHAPTER 2. Accounting for Tactical Innovation and Variety of Nonviolent Tactics

Since Gene Sharp's publication of 198 methods and, in particular, in the last two decades, researchers have noticed an uptick in the frequency of new, nationwide, anti-authoritarian campaigns (Chenoweth and Stephan 2016). Simultaneously, thousands of anti-corruption, pro-climate, and social justice civil resistance campaigns, to mention just a few, began using of a wide range of highly innovative nonviolent tactics.

What can account for this tactical innovation and deployment of such a variety of nonviolent tactics? Some of the contributing factors, described in greater detail below, include:

1. Digital technology: growth and documentation
2. Arts-based and cultural resistance
3. Human rights activism
4. Diffusion of knowledge about civil resistance
5. Tactical innovation from women and sexual/gender minorities
6. Resistance to the rise of global corporate power
7. Ongoing repression
8. Competition for public attention
9. Competition for resources among groups within a movement
10. Natural or human-induced disasters

Digital Technology: Growth and Documentation

The digital revolution has spurred information technologies that promote expression and communication through digital screens, cameras, electronic speakers, and microphones. Governments use some of these tools to concentrate power, such as mass surveillance and databases of social media activity. But citizens also utilize these tools to disperse power and information, and to sous-veil governments.[29]

Mass numbers of people around the world use mobile phones to text, call, and communicate. Social media networks such as Facebook are being increasingly accessed on mobile

---

[29] Sousveillance is defined as recording an activity from the point of view of someone involved, usually by a portable recording device.

devices and have accumulated more than one billion users. Opportunities are ever-present to express disruptive views or make positive appeals, particularly as information transcends geographical boundaries and people are exposed to new political and cultural ideas.

In addition to social media networks, there are a number of major online platforms focused on supporting activism. Avaaz.org, for example, is the largest advocacy organization on the web, with currently upwards of 55 million "members" in 194 countries. Avaaz mobilizes global citizens in 17 languages around topics such as environmental justice, human rights, social justice, and peace issues. It uses electronic petitions and targeted letters as its defining tactics, raises funds for campaigns and humanitarian issues, and crowd-sources new strategies and information. It also mobilizes people to protest in the streets and lobby to challenge governments, corporations, and religious institutions. As an example of its impact, Avaaz claims partial credit for establishing the Brazilian Anti-Corruption Law, based on a petition and thousands of phone calls.

Another example of digital civil resistance is the work of the group Anonymous, a network of online hackers who attack opponents such as governments, corporations, organizations, and private individuals whom they believe are causing harm. Some of the network's targets have included Sony, Hong Kong Police, a "revenge porn" site founder, and the Saudi Arabian government. In addition to redesigning, caricaturing, defacing or graffitiing websites, Anonymous often reveals private information to the public such as phone numbers, addresses, finances, and social media profiles (known as "doxing"). There is much debate about the ethics and effectiveness of doxing and other forms of secretive or mass attacks in the digital world.

Avaaz and Anonymous are just two of thousands of organizations and campaigns using digital technology in innovative ways to protest and transform perceived injustices. For example, with a blast announcement on Twitter calling for action, hundreds or thousands of individuals can take part in a targeted action by overwhelming a business with calls and other communications.

Today, the opportunity to amplify one's message or to quickly coordinate actions is unprecedented. It is not a surprise that multiple large, coordinated protests worldwide (organized repeatedly and rapidly) have occurred during the digital information age. According to the BBC, the 2003 protest against the U.S. war in Iraq mobilized up to 11 million people in 60 countries; climate change protests have frequently mobilized more than 1,000 coordinated same-day actions; within just days of a deadly attack on a French newspaper office, the #JeSuisCharlie hashtag was used more than 5 million times on Twitter; and the 2016 Avaaz.org campaign claimed 6 million signatures for an open Internet. Millions around the world mobilized on online platforms such as Tiktok and joined the "I Can't Breathe" and "Black Lives Matter" protests in the summer of 2020.

With this unprecedented growth in digital methods of civil resistance, various attempts have been made to collect, systematize, and group together a variety of digital resistance tactics. One example is the Civil Resistance 2.0 project. The brainchild of scholar and activist Mary Joyce, Civil Resistance 2.0 is a crowd-sourced effort to explore the possibilities of new technology to expand and update Sharp's original list of nonviolent methods.[30] The initial intention was to focus on the impact of information and communication technologies, but the list was opened up to include any sort of digital or otherwise technological advancement since 1973. The project is housed in a Google Sheet for maximum flexibility. Civil Resistance 2.0 mirrors Sharp's system of classification. Next to the original method, there are columns for 1) technical enhancements to the original, 2) an entirely new take on the method (or "method 2.0"), and 3) speculative creative variations that have not yet been attempted.

Joyce has observed that traditional methods of non-digital resistance can be amplified via the use of new technologies. Examples include live-tweeting events on Twitter, distributing digital recordings of offline speeches, and publishing text transcripts on websites.

Arts-based and Cultural Resistance

Resistance that utilizes arts and culture, including cultural memes, practices and/or traditions, has been an integral part of historical and contemporary nonviolent struggles (Bartkowski, 2013). Some even called this "transformative resistance," a type of "sophisticated struggle which focuses on mind, speech and action to work towards [individual and collective] liberation ..." (Dorjee 2015, 16). This kind of cultural struggle consists of engaging in self-constructive actions in the midst of repression, such as "promoting [...] language and other self-reliance and cultural capital-building activities" (18).

Cultural workers, including artists, musicians, poets, and writers have long played a major role in resistance and social change struggles. They have challenged societal norms and assumptions and used art and cultural memes or traditions explicitly to support civil resistance and social change. Many have used their art to protest, hold powerholders accountable, and appeal for social justice. Their solo activities along with the collective work of orchestras, dance troupes, and mass artistic protest have significantly expanded the repertoire of nonviolent resistance in the cultural sphere, compelling us to create a more systematic approach for categorizing such actions.

The uptick in cultural resistance in North America has been particularly apparent since the protests against the World Trade Organization (WTO) in Seattle in 1999. Enormous puppets

---

30   For more information, see the webinar presentation by Mary Joyce on Civil Resistance 2.0:
       https://www.nonviolent-conflict.org/civil-resistance-2-0-digital-enhancements-to-the-198-nonviolent-methods/

and innumerable props played a central role in the marches and blockades led by protesters. Since then, many large assemblies and protests have been accompanied by art-builds, which are warehouses or spaces that produce large quantities of banners, props, large *papier-mâché* puppets, large-scale balloons of the earth, and stilts. 350.org, a global environmental organization dedicated to stopping climate change, employs a full-time art director and many of its protests are visually and theatrically staged for maximum appeal and attention. The Amplifier Foundation, an "art machine for social change," is entirely dedicated to the production and distribution of art as a means to support grassroots campaigns.

Beautiful Trouble (Boyd and Mitchell, 2016) is a book that highlights effective tactics of creative resistance utilized in many campaigns. It was co-written by scores of activists in the Internet cloud and has an accompanying website, network, and training group that seek to promote effective, creative nonviolent actions.[31] The book's subtitle, A Toolbox for Revolution, describes its purpose accurately, as it is meant to be readily accessible to activists in need of concrete support and advice.

To account for the massive expansion in cultural resistance methods, Bloch (2015), a long-time trainer, artist, and associate of Nonviolence International, has proposed 12 categories of cultural resistance methods (Sharp did not identify or categorize them).

Bloch's cultural resistance tactics include:

1. 2-dimensional arts (graphics/images/words: murals, banners, posters, stickers, comics, caricatures, logos)

2. 3-dimensional arts (puppets, props, objects, costumes, mascots, sculpture)

3. sound/musical arts (drumming, noisemaking, spoken word)

4. theater arts (guerrilla and invisible theaters,[32] traditional, identity correction)

5. movement arts (dance, martial arts, walks, marches, circus arts)

6. media/documentation arts (video, radio, film, archives)

7. literature (newspapers, leaflets, books, poetry)

8. delineation of space (physical spaces/structures which exclude or resist violence/militarization, peace parks/demilitarized zones, peace villages, peace abbies)

---

31 For more information, see: **http://beautifultrouble.org/**.

32 Guerilla theater is when activists put on a surprise public performance that is designed to shock the audience, while invisible theater does not seek to be recognized as such and is presented as reality.

9. cultural institution-building (houses of cultural preservation, native language schools, traditional arts schools)

10. crafts and traditions (clothing, food)

11. rituals (national/spiritual/religious celebrations, funerals)

12. language preservation (linguistic rights activists)

Many of these cultural resistance tactics are primarily artistic and expressive in function. Most cultural and artistic activities are typically performed in commercial settings outside of highly charged social conflicts. When they are intentionally used in a conflict setting to appeal to the public or to protest against opponents, we label them as nonviolent actions.

The first seven categories of cultural resistance tactics listed above have been included in this monograph's updated classification of tactics of expression (see Tables 1 and 4) The cultural resistance tactics in categories 8-12 have anchored or contributed to a form of constructive direct action that this monograph classifies in a self-standing category of constructive intervention. Stellan Vinthagen (2015) refers to these constructive tactics as examples of developing a "nonviolent society's culture of resistance alternatives," as long as they are dually "intervening in relationships of domination and implementing an alternative way of living."[33]

Human Rights Activism

Another reason for the development of new civil resistance tactics relates to the global movement for human rights. In the 1970s, human rights activism and institutions grew in prominence with the support of Amnesty International, Human Rights Watch, the United Nations, and iconic dissident figures of rights-based movements like Solzhenitsyn, Mandela, Havel, and Mothers of the Plaza de Mayo. A powerful new framework for local grassroots activism based on international law has continued to grow, supported by many allies in the international human rights community including labor unions and human rights groups such as Human Rights First PEN, Frontline, and a number of national organizations.

Beyond defense lawyers, human rights defenders now include anyone upholding international laws and conventions, such as journalists and writers defending Article 19 of the UN

---

33 Vinthagen (2015) outlines nine components of nonviolent culture: 1) socialization, 2) socio-material reproduction, 3) cultural reconstruction, 4) movement stories in daily life, 5) movement rituals and ceremonies, 6) free zones, 7) group boundaries, 8) movement-oriented interpretive frameworks, 9) the politicization of daily life.

Declaration for Human Rights, women activists campaigning for gender equality, and indigenous people struggling for survival. Other defenders include minority groups fighting nonviolently for self-determination, political parties demanding free and fair elections, students advocating for universal education, and workers defending labor laws enacted by the International Labor Organization.

International human rights law establishes minimum standards of dignity that governments have voluntarily signed to uphold but often fail to effectively implement. There is now a UN Rapporteur for Human Rights Defenders, as well as a reformed UN Human Rights Council with Universal Periodic Reviews monitoring how member states implement human rights law. The combination of local and international human rights pressure has proved formidable in bringing social change to countries such as Colombia and El Salvador (Wilson, 2017).

The New Tactics in Human Rights (NTHR) database is a valuable resource for human rights defenders. The NTHR is a multi-language site designed to help human rights campaigners deploy tactics used in other campaigns. NTHR has documented hundreds of tactics promoting international legal standards. In many communities, human rights defense has supplanted nonviolent resistance as the major strategic avenue for social change. Human rights defenders traditionally work more closely with the courts and legislatures, seeking to hold them accountable and to uphold their stated ideals. Still, many tactics that human rights defenders deploy, such as vigils and funeral protests, are methods of nonviolent resistance. Some of the examples of nonviolent action harvested from NTHR for the purpose of this monograph are mock tribunals, guerilla lawyering, and the creation of fake money to combat bribery (see Universe of Nonviolent Tactics Appendix).

Diffusion of Knowledge About Civil Resistance

Although a digital divide still exists in many parts of the world, and digital surveillance and censorship are common practices, the Internet has contributed significantly to the worldwide spread of knowledge about civil resistance. Before the Internet, the efforts of scholars, educators, and trainers to teach nonviolent resistance were confined to in-person interaction or telephone calls—and the financial and logistical limitations that came with them. Improved Internet access, both in terms of infrastructure and affordability, as well as connectivity advancements in many parts of the world, has enabled educators to explore less costly and more easily scalable educational avenues. Today, a number of universities and civil society actors offer online, offline, and hybrid courses on nonviolent civil resistance and nonviolent action. Measuring the impact of online courses on participants remains a challenge and is still rather limited. However, refined survey tools are being developed to provide important insights into the short and long-term changes in attitudes, skills, and knowledge of participants as a result of online learning on civil resistance (Bartkowski, 2019).

Documentary films have also served as a powerful educational tool. Documentaries examining cases of civil resistance around the world such as *A Force More Powerful*, *Bringing Down a Dictator*, and *Orange Revolution* have reached tens of millions of viewers. More broadly, one may speak of a sort of "documentary resistance," which, drawing on the work of Bartkowski (2013) and movement historian Jacques Semelin, Amber French (2017) describes as "[e]fforts to document, preserve, and transmit information about past nonviolent movements [as] acts of civil resistance, [including] raw traces of movements (photos, videos, etc.).…." Two primary groups can engage in documentary resistance:

A. Activists/movements, through generating leaflets, posters, videos, leaders' speeches, interviews, and so on.

B. Historians, journalists, documentary directors, and others who write and create films about, and/or study past movements, producing accounts and analysis that today's movements can refer to, consult, and learn from.

The underlying concept of documentary resistance is defying repression (whether in the form of movement repression or of censored historical narratives) so that future movements can learn from the experience and actions of past movements.

Language translation of resources on civil resistance is another important development in the dissemination of knowledge. Sharp's works have been translated into 36 languages, and the ICNC online Resource Library features an extensive and growing list of English-language and translated resources in over 70 languages available for free download.

Information technologies have provided citizens with ways to circumvent communication restrictions established by authoritarian regimes who routinely seek to limit and/or regulate information about resistance campaigns at home and abroad. The use of information technologies to broadcast the 2010-11 protests against Tunisian dictator Zine El Abidine Ben Ali spurred a contagion effect of protests first in Egypt and then throughout the Arab world, known as the Arab Spring.

With the diffusion of knowledge about nonviolent actions across regions, countries, and communities, there is greater potential for reflective learning that spurs tactical innovation and helps wage nonviolent campaigns more creatively and effectively.

Tactical Innovation from Women and Sexual/Gender Minorities

Women and girls have been deeply engaged in many nonviolent campaigns throughout history, often displaying strong tactical innovation and creativity. While men have often used mass violence in conflicts, women have mostly waged conflict through nonviolent action. According to scholars Mary Elizabeth King and Anne-Marie Codur:

> Women pioneered many of the hundreds of nonviolent methods that have been observed throughout history... Women activists have been able to capitalize on five sociological features that gave them an edge and a specific advantage in civil resistance movements, compared to men:
>
> 1. Women's presence lowers the level of violence and repression from security forces.
> 2. Women are often the best keepers of nonviolent discipline inside the movement.
> 3. Women tend to organize in horizontal networks, which prove to be more efficient and resilient for a movement than male-run hierarchical systems.
> 4. Women display fewer internal rivalries and can frequently achieve greater unity than male activists.
> 5. Women show a greater ability than men to build ties of solidarity across and beyond societal lines of division (be they religious, ethnic, or socio-economic) and political rivalries. (Kurtz and Kurtz, 2015, 433).

Historically, women have championed dispersed mass actions such as boycotts and expressive protests. The *cacerolazo* form of protest, which consists of banging on pots and pans as part of a march or similar event, was invented by women and used in dispersed actions in repressive places.

Yet many women-led nonviolent struggles using concentrated tactics have also left their mark on history. Since the early 2000s, Women of Zimbabwe Arise (WOZA) has participated in the annual "March for Love" on St. Valentine's Day, campaigning to end torture and authoritarian rule. In the 1970s and 80s, the Mothers of the Plaza de Mayo in Argentina catalyzed mass protests and citizen mobilization by holding a public vigil with portraits of their disappeared children.

Women's capacity for tactical innovation has time and again transcended restrictive gender roles. Many women have risen up to exploit these societal expectations to their own strategic advantage. King and Codur argue that traditional gender roles can offer women:

... a strategic advantage, because they allow them to function within customary stereotypes while utilizing the tools that can be employed as weapons against certain aspects of the society's patriarchal structures... As they challenged the authorities in the name of those "superior" family values, as good wives and devoted mothers, they were able to create powerful, irresistible dilemma actions.

At the same time, there are numerous examples of women engaging in civil disobedience *against* restrictive, gender-based laws and cultural expectations in societies around the world. Examples include wearing pants instead of skirts and dresses, voting, driving vehicles, participating in a non-conforming marriage, smoking cigarettes, making legal contracts, and refusing *sati* (self-immolation of widows).

Furthermore, the evolution of modern gender roles in many regions of the world has opened up new resistance horizons for women in professional, social, and political arenas. Women have run underground abortion and medical clinics in numerous countries. In Liberia in 2003, women exposed their nude bodies in public in a successful effort to shame men and pressure them to sign a cease-fire agreement. In Burkina Faso in 2014, women played a prominent role in resisting dictatorship by "emerging from their homes, waving spatulas in the air—a rare sign of disapproval in Burkinabé culture which signaled to others across the country the degree of seriousness the resistance was reaching" (Zunes 2017).

Importantly, King and Codur, as well as Marie Principe (2016) point out the regenerative and reinforcing effects that women's nonviolent organizing and mobilization have had for broader struggles in many societies. For example, the women's petition movement of Iran in 2006 served as a foundation for the 2009 Green Revolution. Conversely, women's leadership in the U.S. civil rights movement helped catalyze feminist tactics of the 1970s and later decades, including decentralized affinity-group based mobilizations, de-genderizing bathrooms, breast-feeding in public, creating women-centered religious groups and rituals, and using non-sexist language.

In the 20th century, gay, bisexual, and lesbian people publicly broke gender norms by romantically and sexually loving people of the same sex. This has led to all sorts of resistance such as kiss-ins, gay and lesbian sex, erotica and pornography, underground pharmacies, and cross-dressing protests. Tactical innovations included handcuffing oneself to live news broadcasters, running underground pharmacies, throwing glitter, and developing the rainbow flag as an identity symbol.

Understanding civil resistance tactics through a gender lens remains a relatively unexplored area. More research is needed to identify and document the contributions of gender and sexual minorities, including transgender people, intersex individuals, and many others, to nonviolent resistance in general and tactical innovation in civil resistance, specifically.

Resistance to the Rise of Global Corporate Power

For hundreds of years, a driving force behind economic globalization has been transnational corporations (TNCs). These entities were backed by European powers during colonial times and, in modern times, they have been supported by world powers such as the United States and China as well as former colonial powers such as France and the United Kingdom, among others. TNCs dominate local governance, which can have harmful effects on multiple levels of society, particularly in countries with weak governance. Examples of TNCs currently in operation include oil companies Shell in Nigeria, Total in Burma, and Hunt Oil in Peru; gold extraction companies Freeport-McMoRan in West Papua and Centerra Gold in Kyrgyzstan; and timber extraction companies operating in the Congo Basin, the Amazon Basin, and in various Southeast Asian countries.

Relatively weak local communities with little leverage over powerful TNCs obtain few tax revenues or profits from resource extraction and are stuck with the long-term health and environmental costs. Most of the related nonviolent campaigns that local communities lead, often with international allies, have been focused on strategic frame that has driven tactical innovation called **points of intervention** (as identified in the quote below). Effective opposition to these global firms has required a global response, facilitated by modern communication and travel. As noted by Patrick Reinsborough and Doyle Canning (2008) at StoryBasedStrategy.org:

> *[tactical] interventions come at many places—from the* **point of destruction** *where resource extraction is devastating intact ecosystems, indigenous lands, and local communities, to the* **point of production** *where workers are organizing in the sweatshops and factories of the world. Solidarity actions spring up at the* **point of consumption** *where the products that are made from unjust processes are sold, and inevitably communities of all types take direct actions at the* **point of decision** *to confront the decision makers who have the power to make the changes they need.*

Another common intervention occurrence comes at the **point of transportation** in the form of blockades of ships, trains, and other vehicles.

Greenpeace and Indonesian campaigners have been working to preserve rainforests from palm oil plantations. In addition to direct efforts to halt logging, activists have also tried to blockade ports, blockade palm oil factories, promote boycotts of palm-oil products, and organize protests aiming to pressure palm oil executives (Schlegel, 2016).

Environmentalists have innovated at the point of destruction through the use of tripod blockades in which a large tripod device is set up on roads or in front of properties and a single person climbs to the top of the device. The tripod cannot be moved without risking serious harm to the person. A single device and one person can be used to block a large expanse which makes this tactic quite efficient.

Another innovation is identity correction as practiced by the Yes Men, who impersonate corporate executives who "apologize" and "offer reparations" for transgressions such as the Bopal industrial accident. Dow, the accident perpetrator, chose to quickly disavow that apology and reparations offer—an act that caused further reputation damage. Anti-whaling groups have intervened non-lethally with whaling harvesters by shining laser light at whalers, to interpose between the whales and the poachers, to chase and shadow whalers and seize and damage drift nets at sea. Given the ubiquity of transnational corporation activities and the lack of international laws and mechanisms to rein in their power, civil resistance campaigners have expanded their repertoire of methods to intervene accordingly.

Ongoing Repression

Authoritarian regimes routinely repress and retaliate against the independent actions of civil societies and are constantly inventing and experimenting with new means of doing so (Burrows and Stephan 2015). This authoritarian pushback tends to spur tactical innovation on the part of repressed but still mobilized groups. Authorities are not prepared for this. To minimize the costs as well as risks of being repressed, activists are incentivized to experiment with a variety of nonviolent resistance tactics.

In response to the Chinese government's attempts to censor Internet "speech" by banning the use of specific words, netizens relentlessly invent new homophones and homonyms to communicate important information and to support free speech (Shaou and Dodge 2017). In another creative response to repression, the Sahrawi people abandoned the capital city of Laayoune in 2010 in a mass protest against Moroccan occupation of their region and built an alternative tent city. The Moroccan government eventually destroyed the tent city. Sahrawi activists responded to the repression and the ban on *kheimas* (the traditional nomad tents and the platforms of social life) by pitching them on the roofs of their homes. In Hong Kong in 2019, citizens formed a symbolic 32 kilometers of human chain, held up thank you signs to many foreign supporters, and deployed the mass use of laser pointing in response to police repression.

Competition for Public Attention

Movements often engage in competition for the public's attention through mainstream news media. Campaigns also compete in "bandwidth" with business and charity sector advertising. The frequent desire to be noticed by the mainstream news, combined with the understanding that the same repetitive actions can fade in their effectiveness and newsworthiness over time, drives some movements in a relentless creative process and search for "new" attention-grabbing actions.

People for the Ethical Treatment of Animals (PETA) is famous for its motto, "All news is good news." This motto suggests that even controversial actions that may anger many in the public, such as throwing blood on people wearing fur coats, or disrobing, are successful because they garner publicity and raise awareness about a grievance. Most movements do not subscribe to this extreme strategy of attention-getting, but some do.

Competition for Resources among Groups within a Movement

Cunningham, Dahl, and Fruge (2017) statistically analyzed the diffusion and diversification of tactics used in self-determination struggles from 1975 to 2005 and found that: "Given limitations on their capabilities, competition among organizations in a shared movement, and different resource requirements for nonviolent strategies, we show that organizations have incentives to diversify tactics rather than just copy other organizations."

They statistically demonstrated that when some organizations use resource-intensive methods such as boycotts or mass protests that are successful, others are incentivized to copy them. However, in many cases, activists try less resource-intensive tactics such as a blockade or an online petition. Internal competition for resources, the impact of tactics, and public support for using specific tactics all drive creativity and diversification of tactics.

One campaign was able to achieve an impact with a less resource-intensive tactic called maptivism. This method was developed in conjunction with the women's rights campaign in Egypt and resulted in the 2015 creation of Harassmap, an interactive app that displays crowd-sourced reports of harassment on a map. This tactic required only a few app developers working as volunteers and willing citizens to report incidents. In Tunisia in 2011, one group initiated an online campaign of self-portraits of individuals holding signs reading "Enough Ali" to protest then President Zine El Abidine Ben Ali. These photographs were collated online in a mosaic fashion to demonstrate the enormous number of Tunisians who were calling for the president's removal.

Natural or Human-induced Disasters

Pandemics and ecological disasters are not new to humanity. However, the change in scale, severity and speed of these disasters has generated new opportunities for tactical innovation. The 2020 COVID pandemic is an example of a disaster which led to numerous tactical innovations. For example, KPop fans on Tiktok flooded the Trump Campaign with ticket requests to his Oklahoma rally, in order to deprive his supporters of the opportunity to attend the rally and to mislead the organizers about the number of attendees. California activists deployed a virtual (decentralized) art build, photographing their work which was stitched together to spell a message. Millions of people produced face masks on home sewing machines and communities mobilized to collect and distribute protective equipment without government support. In Honduras, activists turned bank notes into face masks as a symbol of their demands for government transparency. Online rallies for numerous causes were held.[34]

The points in this section are not exhaustive but instead aim to explore some of the dominant trends in tactical innovation. Given the deployment of nonviolent tactics in an array of civil resistance movements, in all countries and in most sectors of modern societies, there are surely other factors that are driving the use of new nonviolent methods and the tactical innovation of old ones.

---

[34] For more information, see: Chenoweth, Erica, and Jeremy Pressman. "Collective Action & Dissent under COVID: Crowd Counting Consortium." Google Sites, 2020. **https://sites.google.com/view/crowdcountingconsortium/dissent-under-covid**.

CHAPTER 3. Categorizing Nonviolent Tactics

This chapter starts with an overview of Gene Sharp's work on nonviolent methods because of its significance and popularity. It then adds insights from Ebert, Gandhi, Bond, Bloch, and others to synthesize a more inclusive classification system of nonviolent tactics.

The chapter concludes by presenting alternative research and ideas for classifying tactics such as those proposed by Beyerle, Vinthagen, and others, with the hope that this area of civil resistance study may be more fully integrated into our understanding of old and new tactics and how activists use them.

Sharp's Classification of Nonviolent Methods

Sharp may not have been the first to begin identifying nonviolent methods, but he was the first to begin systematically documenting them. In the 1950s, Sharp identified and catalogued various types of nonviolent resistance methods that he came across through a painstaking review of numerous historical conflicts and movements. After first compiling a list of nonviolent tactics, which he called methods, he attempted to classify them systematically. Sharp developed a typology that organized this complex field of human behavior into three distinct categories of resistance: A) protest and persuasion, B) noncooperation, and C) intervention. These categories have proven durable and yet are flexible enough to easily include newly emerging methods.

A. Protest and persuasion tactics are group actions designed primarily to "say" or express protester grievances and demands. This category commonly includes assemblies, processions, theater performances, public speeches, puppets, petitions, videos, and virtual marches. Protest and persuasion convey the two primary purposes of expressive action: to communicate what a movement is campaigning "for" and what a movement is campaigning "against." However, "persuasion" can be misconstrued to imply that actions that do not succeed in persuading an adversary don't satisfy the definition of a nonviolent method. In this monograph, we call this functional method "appeal" which has a more unilateral meaning.

B. Noncooperation tactics are acts of "not doing" and typically operate by withdrawing cooperation from opponents. Sharp collected and categorized 100 different kinds of noncooperation methods and divided them into three subcategories: social, economic, and political. Social noncooperation includes ostracizing people, suspending social and sports activities, staying at home, and collective disappearance. Economic noncooperation includes 25 forms of boycotts (refusal to buy) and 22 forms of strikes (refusal to sell). Political noncooperation includes citizen and civil servant noncooperation with government, noncooperation actions by states, and tactics such as slow compliance, disguised disobedience, hiding, and civil disobedience of laws considered illegitimate.

C. Intervention tactics are generally disruptive acts of "doing" that seek to physically or psychologically interfere with opponents' actions or manipulate the conditions. These include nonviolent land seizures, reverse trials,[35] subvertising,[36] tree sits, and guerrilla theater. This category also includes tactics that develop alternative institutions and social norms and practices such as alternative markets, transportation, communications systems, social institutions, and parallel governments.

Sharp's classification system also designates numerous sub-categories of methods. Some sub-categories refer to arenas of action (social intervention) or specific actors (economic noncooperation on the part of workers and producers). Others point to intentions (pressure on individuals, honoring the dead) or the material medium used (drama, music). However, the methods of nonviolent action are highly diverse and context-driven, making it difficult to subcategorize them effectively and consistently. For example, Sharp's sub-categories of protest and persuasion are particularly eclectic. Table 4 attempts to catalogue these methods more consistently by grouping them according to the medium in which they are conducted: digital technology, material arts, the human body, or language.

Sharp's definition of tactics has a few drawbacks. Some identified methods might not easily fit into one category because they involve a mixture of doing, not doing, and saying something. Sharp also equates his nonviolent methods with military weapons used against an adversary and, in doing so, excludes many actions that engage society but do not directly target a movement's adversary. Excluded from Sharp's methods are, for example, constructive actions such as educational, advocacy, and organizational efforts designed to pull support and loyalty away from the opponent and enhance the social cohesion and self-organization of the repressed society. In reality, most campaign successes are determined by obtaining majority support (rather than unanimous support) from society or other stakeholders; conversion of leading opponents rarely happens. Another drawback is his decision to ignore categorical distinctions between coercive and persuasive methods.

Sharp also warned against inferring that there is a ready-made template for selecting and sequencing his identified categories of tactics to execute successful nonviolent struggles. By and large, however, the simplicity of Sharp's classification system has been instrumental

---

35 Reverse trials are defined as courtroom trials where the accused assumes the role of a prosecutor putting on trial a law, policy, or an issue (Sharp 1973).

36 Subvertising is defined as co-opting an advertisement for a subversive or originally unintended goal.

in its popularity among activists and near-universal adoption among civil resistance trainers, teachers, writers, and scholars.

Keeping in mind Sharp's enduring classification typology, what follows is an overview of other ways civil resistance practitioners and analysts classify tactics, all of which inform the universal framework developed in this monograph (Tables 1 and 4).

Disruptive and Constructive Resistance

No discussion of nonviolent tactics is complete without recognizing the central contributions of Mohandas Gandhi. Gandhi invented much of what we consider modern-day nonviolent action. He coined and popularized many of the field's terms, practices, and philosophies. Gandhi called his overarching philosophy *satyagraha* (by which he meant civil resistance). He strongly believed in the importance of consistency between the vision of a new India and the means it deployed to achieve those goals, including maintaining empathy for its opponents, the British. Persuasion, nonviolent coercion, and constructive action were all strategies that he deployed at various stages of the pro-independence struggle (Ackerman and DuVall 2000; Cortright 2008; Sharp 1979).

Gandhi is well-known for his use of hunger strikes, utilizing the dramatic and contentious nature of these fasts to draw attention to his concerns. He often used this method to induce cooperation from other members of the Indian independence movement, in addition to pressuring the British government. His support for economic boycotts of British goods had a strong coercive impact on British society and the British government. These, along with tactics such as filling the jails and overwhelming the judicial system, are examples of disruptive and confrontational actions.

Gandhi coined the popular term "constructive program" to describe his efforts to improve the lives and discipline of his peers, as well as to strengthen their self-reliance. Through the use of cotton weaving, agricultural ashrams, and salt-making, and the development of new social norms to reduce caste and gender barriers, Gandhi attempted to lay the foundation for Indians to build alternative social and economic institutions to serve as competition to the oppressive British system.

As part of constructive actions, Gandhi also practiced the unusual tactic of unilateral rewards. For example, Gandhi called off (active abstention) a mass march on January 1, 1914 in South Africa, because of an unrelated railway strike. He stated that his campaign did not want to take advantage of the weakness of the government hit by the ongoing strike. The British responded favorably to this unilateral goodwill gesture and entered into negotiations which produced an agreement that gave Indians limited civil rights. Unilateral rewards or offers are unusual in contentious conflict.

Constructive resistance was practiced well before Gandhi—for example, in the 18th century American colonial struggle against the British (Conser, McCarthy, Toscano and Sharp 1986). Some researchers have also highlighted the role of routine, constructive actions in resistance. Bartkowski (2011), for example, showed that this type of action was part of the repertoire of nonviolent resistance that strengthened the social fabric of the emerging Polish nation in the late 19th century and built up cultural and economic institutions that proved instrumental in re-establishing the Polish state after World War I. Polish families sent their children to Polish language schools, often at some political or economic cost to them, to strengthen Polish identity, shared narratives, communication, and social bonds. Such daily actions made up a constructive program of cultural, linguistic, and socio-economic organizing, which was disruptive to the German, Austrian, and Russian authorities. Bartkowski (2011), along with Burrowes (1994), sub-classifies these constructive methods as creative interventions that are distinct from disruptive interventions, such as blockades and hunger strikes.

A challenge in classifying constructive actions is differentiating between inward-oriented actions and outward-oriented (direct) actions. Inward-oriented constructive actions are designed primarily to strengthen internal cohesion and skills of a resisting group or a campaign, such as educational activities and training. Outward-oriented constructive actions, such as persuasive pray-ins or Indians making salt in colonial India, intend to directly induce an opponent to change their actions or even worldviews.

This monograph incorporates into its analysis outward-focused constructive actions that challenge an opponent via persuasion or coercion, or both, and excludes from its analysis constructive actions aiming internally to build or strengthen a movement, as they fall more into training and capacity-building activities and out of the scope of this analysis.

Ebert's Categorization of Nonviolent Tactics

Subsequent to Mohandas Gandhi, Clarence Marsh Case (1923), Krishnalal Shridharani (1939), Joan Bondurant (1958), and Anthony de Crespigny (1964) were among the first to formulate an understanding of nonviolent tactics. Theodore Ebert (1970) built on their work and developed a robust collection of different forms of nonviolent action and a theory on how these methods work. He classified nonviolent methods as either confrontational or constructive. According to Ebert, confrontational actions are intended to stop or reverse an opponent's actions; constructive actions are persuasive or innovative in nature and intended to build a just order in society.

Confrontational actions include:

- protests (flyers and marches);
- legal noncooperation (boycotts and slow-down strikes); and
- civil disobedience (tax refusal and general strike).

Constructive actions include:

- presenting alternatives (seminars);
- legal innovative activities (founding educational institutions, newspapers, and mutual aid societies); and
- civil usurpation (invasions, takeovers, and self-governing bodies). Ebert posits that civil usurpation actions are used in increasingly forceful phases or stages.

TABLE 3: Ebert's Classification System (1970)

Stage of escalation	NATURE OF ACTION		How it works
	CONFRONTATIONAL ACTION Actions that are directed against injustice in society	**CONSTRUCTIVE ACTION** Actions that help construct a just order in society	
1. Actions that bring the issue into the public arena	**Protest** (Demonstration, petition, leafleting, vigil)	**Presenting alternatives** (Teach-in, lectures, show alternative)	Publicizing/ convincing
2. Legal actions that deal with the issue	**Legal noncooperation** (Strike, consumer boycott, go-slow)	**Legal innovative activities** (Fair trade, free school, alternative economy, ethical investment, nonviolent intervention)	Raising the stakes (costs) and minimizing the rewards for those committing injustice
3. Illegal actions that deal with the issue	**Civil disobedience** (Sit-in, blockade, tax resistance, strike, war resistance)	**Civil usurpation** (Sanctuary movement, pirate radio, reverse strike, nonviolent intervention)	Redirecting power

Ebert argues that tactics are usually deployed in a manner that matches an ideal strategic escalation. He claims that in the early phases of a campaign, activists typically use methods designed to publicize a problem and persuade people that change is necessary, in order to put an issue on the public agenda. His second stage of escalation comprises legal actions that are intended to raise the costs for an opponent. In his third phase of escalation, Ebert states that illegal (direct) actions are both contentious and coercive and result in redirecting power. This means that the collective actors are using tactics to actually shape new power relations and relationships.

Another contribution to understanding nonviolent methods is Ebert's focus on how nonviolent action works. He argues that expressive activities seek to publicize and convince; that legal actions to control resources are intended to raise the costs and minimize rewards for an adversary; and lastly that activists' illegal actions to control resources aim to redirect and usurp power. Grouping methods by how they work has strongly influenced our understanding and classification of methods.

One of the biggest challenges with Ebert's distinction between legal and illegal actions is the fact that laws vary by locale. A sit-down strike may be legal in one country, but the same act could be illegal in another and therefore categorized differently. Furthermore, Ebert's emphasis on stages can be misinterpreted as prescriptive. In reality, campaigns can begin in stage two or stage three and certain actions may be more escalatory in stage one than in stage two or three. This study and the Nonviolent Tactics Database incorporate Ebert's dualistic categorization of nonviolent tactics into confrontational and constructive groups (see Table 3).

Mechanisms of Nonviolent Direct Action

Mechanisms of nonviolent direct action[37] are yet another categorization of tactics focused specifically on how the tactics work. Bond (1994) identifies three relevant mechanisms of nonviolent direct action: discrete manipulation, public coercion, and demonstrative appeals.

1. Discrete manipulation refers to the "ability to control resources," such as mobilizing people for a protest or organizing a trucker strike to block roads with vehicles.

2. Public coercion primarily refers to threats or imposed costs to another's interests.[38] For example, this could include the threat of a citizen arrest of a political or corporate

---

37　Mechanisms of direct nonviolent action are often confused with the mechanisms of change described earlier in this monograph. Mechanisms of change are how a movement's opponent reacts to a successful tactic or campaign. Mechanisms of direct action, in turn, refer to the underlying processes by which methods of action operate to affect change in a conflict situation.

38　Bond (1994) mentions another mechanism of direct action: physical force. It usually operates with public coercion to affect the will of an opponent. However, without coercion, it operates through displacement (physically moving the opponent), incapacitation (injuring the opponent), or elimination (killing the opponent). The target is the opponent's body, as opposed to mind. While moving an opponent can be considered nonviolent, injuring or killing an opponent is clearly not.

leader. It also could include shutting down factories through a worker occupation or stay-away.

3. Demonstrative appeals are authoritative, persuasive, or altruistic appeals to shared logic, identity, or ideals directed toward an adversary to influence its will or preferences.

Bond's focus on mechanisms clarifies the relationship between an instance of direct action (or tactic) and its functional purpose. The purpose of political action is to affect the will of opponents (and ultimately their interests) through appeals (incentives) or coercion or physically manipulating the environment. Walking a dog or cooking a meal in most contexts does not manipulate the environment, appeal, or coerce, and therefore does not constitute nonviolent action. However, when Buddhist monks in Burma refused alms (food) that military leaders offered them by turning their bowls upside-down, this simple coercive action was widely believed to threaten the leaders' ability to obtain merit for their afterlife and thus undermined their legitimacy as devout Buddhists.

Categorizing Based on Constructive/Persuasive and Confrontational/Coercive Inducements

Bond expands on Ebert's categorization of constructive (persuasive) tactics (see Table 3) when he introduces three types of appeals:

A. Convincing appeals that invoke a common set of assumptions, rules, logic, or evidence,

B. Authoritative appeals that invoke mutual authority from which legitimacy is drawn, and

C. Altruistic appeals that invoke a common identity.

Additional positive inducements where resisters try to invoke common interests with opponents to affect their will can include:

D. Social, material, or political rewards that benefit another party, or

E. Constructive program, which constructs alternative behaviors, practices, or institutions, or takes over existing institutions, to better or more equitably fulfill societal needs and attract defections and loyalty from the opponent and its allies.

Convincing (A), authoritative (B), and altruistic (C) communication constitute the constructive or persuasive inducements in the monograph's category of tactics known as appeals.

Social, material, or political rewards (D) are the constructive or persuasive inducements in the monograph's category of tactics called refraining. Constructive program (E) falls within the constructive or persuasive inducements for the monograph's category of creative intervention. See Table 1 and Figure 1.

FIGURE 1: Constructive or Persuasive Tactics

In juxtaposition to these positive inducements, this monograph characterizes negative—confrontational or coercive—inducements as the use of threats (F) or the imposition of costs (G) (e.g., social, political, psychological, or economic costs).[39] They fall under the monograph's categories of tactics such as protest, noncooperation, and disruptive intervention as presented in Figure 2 and adopted in Table 1.

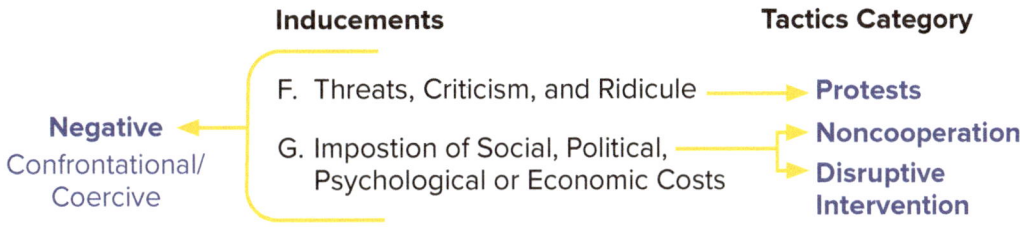

FIGURE 2: Confrontational or Coercive Tactics

---

39   Coercive methods can use violent or nonviolent threats and negative sanctions. With physical coercion, the body is targeted to influence the will or mind of the opponent. Except for the narrow use of physical force, all the mechanisms of direct action operate through social power, i.e., through the will of others.

Bond's categorization informs the universe of civil resistance tactics introduced in this monograph to the extent that the nonviolent actions (saying, not-doing, doing or creating) include either coercion or persuasion or both.

Kreisberg (1998) proposes a slightly different connection between methods and outcomes in his studies on what he refers to as "constructive conflict." He identifies three classes of methods: persuasion, coercion, and reward. Like Bond, Burrowes, and others, Kreisberg focuses on the importance of affecting another's will. He argues that nonviolent (social) power operates through the will of others by affecting their interests (which may be symbolic, material, social, political, or economic) and involves tangible costs, threats, rewards, or risks to the opponent. Kriesberg's persuasion is akin to Bond's appeal, which seeks to convince or sway another party's mind or will through logic and reason. Kreisberg includes reward as an inducement, whether through a bribe (though civil resisters would usually not consider this because it would contradict their anti-corruption messages) or a generous offer at the negotiating table.

Although rare in civil resistance conflicts, unilateral rewards matching movement strategies and visions are used. For example, in Armenia on May 2, 2018, the opposition to the ruling party launched a general strike that forced the nation to a halt for one day. Protests were unilaterally suspended until May 8, when a successful parliamentary vote for the opposition to take power was held.

Bond and Kreisberg share an analysis of mechanisms and inducements of nonviolent action that are grounded in positive "constructive" sanctions (appeals, persuasion, rewards) and negative "confrontational" sanctions (nonviolent threats and coercion). They are also framed in similar terms by Ebert's (1970) "confrontational and constructive action" and Barbara Deming's (1971) "two hands of nonviolence."[40] This monograph adopts this dualistic understanding of the confrontational/coercive and constructive/persuasive inducements of nonviolent action.

---

40 In her book, *On Revolution and Equilibrium* (1971), Barbara Deming presents the metaphor of the two hands of nonviolence: "On the one hand (symbolized by a hand firmly stretched out and signaling, 'Stop!') I will not cooperate with your violence or injustice; I will resist it with every fiber of my being. And, on the other hand (symbolized by the hand with its palm turned open and stretched toward the other) I am open to you as a human being" (16).

Alternative Classifications of Nonviolent Tactics

Researchers created alternative classifications of tactics in light of specific nonviolent struggles, including campaigns or movements a) against occupation, b) for civil defense, c) fighting corruption, and d) against institutional and class domination.

Civil Resistance Against Occupation

Andrew Rigby uses a unique typology of nonviolent tactics to analyze the Palestinian struggle (Rigby 2010; Darweish and Rigby 2015). These categories of tactics include:

- Symbolic resistance: I remain what I was and communicate to others by means of gestures, actions, or dress continued allegiance to my cause and its values.

- Polemical resistance: I oppose the occupier by voicing my protest and trying to encourage others of the need to maintain the struggle.

- Offensive resistance: I am prepared to do all that I can to frustrate and overcome the oppressor by nonviolent means, including strikes, demonstrations, and other forms of direct action.

- Defensive resistance: I aid and protect those in danger or on the run, and thereby preserve human life and human values endangered by the occupying power.

- Constructive resistance: I challenge the existing imposed order by seeking to create alternative institutions that embody the values that I hope to see flourish more widely once we are free. (3)

Rigby's categories of methods are perhaps more suited to occupied peoples. A small improvement to his framing of methods would be to substitute "I" for "we," since collective resistance is the central organizing principle. These categories re-arrange existing tactics of nonviolent resistance, rather than identify new tactics.

Civil Defense

Anders Boserup and Andrew Mack (1975) classify methods of nonviolent action based on their strategic function in civil defense against foreign invasion, occupation, and internal coups as: a) symbolic, b) denial, and c) undermining. Schock (2015a, 8) explains their analysis as follows:

- "Symbolic actions demonstrate unity and strength, define the challengers as a moral community, and force the uncommitted to take a stand.

- Denial actions deprive the opponent of what is taken through coercion or accumulated through exploitative or illegitimate exchange relations.

- Undermining actions attempt to exacerbate or exploit the divisions among opponents and inhibit the cooperation of third parties with opponents."

The functional analysis of Boserup and Mack's classification system has utility beyond strategic defense; it also applies to campaigns for social change. Boserup and Mack's (1975) expansive definition also includes indirect actions against an opponent (such as engagement methods explained by Beyerle below).

Civil Resistance Against Corruption

Beyerle (2014) has pioneered analysis on how civil resistance curtails corruption. She has documented many nonviolent campaigns and methods against corruption, including a campaign against the mafia in Sicily, social audits in Kenya and Afghanistan, and a campaign against corrupt politicians in South Korea. The tactics she identified can be categorized into three functional categories: disruption, engagement, and empowerment.

- Disruptive tactics confront and constrain an adversary. Examples of disruptive methods include information gathering, citizen inspections, festivals, games, and exposing corruption through SMS, e-petitions, and online banners.

- Engagement tactics pull people (and various sectors) toward the campaign and, in some cases, shift loyalties to produce defections, strengthen citizen participation, and weaken corrupt adversaries or their enablers. Engagement can also mean joining forces with institutional activists, such as politicians or civil servants. Examples of engagement methods include negotiation, press conferences, citizen contributions of money and resources, citizen-powerholder meetings, solidarity activities, accompaniment, and displaying resistance symbols on T-shirts, hats, ribbons, and so on.

- Empowerment tactics "shift power relations through the power of numbers," (Beyerle 2014, 32) such that widespread participation generates palpable and un-ignorable social pressure. Examples include trainings, civic education, and coalition and alliance building.

Beyerle's tactics typology differs from the standard classification of nonviolent tactics in two ways. On the one hand, anti-corruption methods include tactical support activities that are not typically direct actions against an opponent in other conflicts. Beyerle argues that training and funds solicitation, for example, serve as nonviolent weapons because they can activate a neutral/passive citizenry, not just serve as a logistical support activity in advance of a rally. In addition, every coin donated to the opposition is one less coin available to the adversary.

Beyerle describes a phenomenon that emphasizes the powerful, central role of disruption, engagement, and empowerment actions directed toward the passive and compliant public in which there is no clear opponent or, if there is one, a large population that is neutral or itself corrupted. Alternatively, anti-corruption methods are often a mix of nonviolent resistance with electioneering, lobbying, and legal fights that advance specific dynamics of nonviolent conflict, e.g., eliciting defections and magnifying backfire potential.[41] In addition to formal processes, anti-corruption campaigns can include routine activities such as negotiation, civic education, and advertising activities.

The embedding of formal and routine actions in anti-corruption campaigns blurs the distinction between more traditional means of influencing politics and non-institutionalized and disruptive civil resistance actions. The categorization framework in this monograph does not include some of Beyerle's anti-corruption methods in order to maintain a clear separation between formal (institutionalized) and informal (extra-institutional) means of waging conflict.

Tactical support activities—single or routine actions that enable a tactic to succeed—are not considered in this monograph to be weapons or tools that directly target an adversary through persuasion, coercion, or manipulation. As such, these types of support activities are not included in this monograph's analysis. For a detailed list of support activities and related information, see page 64.

Everyday Resistance Against Structural and Institutional Dominance

Vinthagen and Johansson (2013), drawing on the works of theorists like Michel Foucault and James C. Scott, have documented an under-examined form of civil resistance: "everyday resistance." They characterize everyday resistance as "quiet, dispersed, disguised, or otherwise seemingly invisible" (4).

They consider everyday resistance, which can encompass attitudes, habits, conversational behaviors, and actions, to constitute an important and undervalued repertoire of civil resistance struggles. Using Foucault's truism that "where there is power, there is resistance" as a starting point, Vinthagen and Johansson have argued that many everyday actions and behaviors constitute resistance to power structures; they are subtle, often unintentional or unsuccessful, and are incorporated into normal social life. Methods of micro, disguised, and hidden resistance include squatting, foot-dragging, desertion, feigned ignorance, or evasion. For example, rather than organizing a mass land occupation, resisters may encroach slowly upon a property. Instead of a mass soldier strike, a steady trickle of daily desertions or deliberate bureaucratic inefficiencies can achieve a similar result in breaking down or slowing military capability.

---

41   See more on backfire in "Basics of Civil Resistance" section of the monograph.

Scott (1989, 27) documents four categories of disguised resistance:

- Everyday resistance methods to material domination including theft, evasion, and foot dragging (see "Everyday Resistance" subsection below for more on the debate surrounding criminality).

- Hidden transcripts of anger, aggression, and a discourse of dignity in response to humiliation or disprivilege. An example of this can be tales of revenge passed from one generation to the next.

- Development of a dissident subculture combating ideological domination through use of tactics such as folk religion, myths of social banditry, and class heroes.

- Direct rebellious action by disguised resisters.

A few methods of everyday resistance are included in this monograph's catalogue of civil resistance (squatting, silence, popular non-obedience, spreading rumors, ID correction with gender markers, etc.). However, this monograph primarily focuses on tactics that aim for social and political goals and are explicitly nonviolent.

"Power-Breaking" Categorization

Vinthagen (2015) proposed a range of tactics of "strategic nonviolence" that he calls the "power-breaking" component of nonviolent resistance.

These include:

1. Counter-discourse: Communicating with well-supported counter-arguments and counter-images (discursive strategies) that disrupt the power's propaganda (fact-finding, symbolism, countering enemy images by counter-behavior, e.g., nonviolent clowning).

2. Competition: Creating alternative and competing nonviolent institutions (in cultural, political, and economic areas).[42]

3. Noncooperation with the existing system's roles or functions (including boycotts) combined with cooperation with people who focus on legitimate and mutual needs (such as relief work during a natural catastrophe).

---

42   Vinthagen uses the term "competition" essentially as a power contestation to reflect elements of what Gandhi called the constructive program. An example he offers is from the Kosovar pro-independence struggle in the 1990s, in which local government services, such as trash pickup and education, were organized as an alternative service in competition with the official Serbian government.

4. Withdrawal: Removing oneself from destructive power relations (flight and the creation of free zones).

5. Hindrance: Stopping or preventing the processes of oppressive power systems (blockades, occupations, and interventions).

6. Dramatizing injustices with humor (self-irony, redefinition, and shock).

7. The strength of this categorization is that it is grounded in the common practices of many nonviolent campaigns and can thus resonate with many activists and campaigners. Vinthagen's method categories are represented in this monograph's framework by **protest and appeal** (encompassing his identified expressive and dramaturgical methods, including counter-discourse methods); **noncooperation and refraining** (encompassing his withdrawal and noncooperation methods); **disruptive intervention** (equivalent to Vinthagen's hindrance methods); and **creative intervention** (encompassing his competition methods). Vinthagen's categorizations are not well known but they are a useful way of classifying nonviolent tactics. See Tables 1 and 4 for relevant examples.

This chapter cites a number of efforts at categorizing nonviolent tactics that put important foundations underneath the monograph's own analysis of the universe of nonviolent tactics. Consequently, the monograph builds on Sharp's categories and integrates elements from Ebert (confrontational and constructive action), Bond (appeals), Kriesberg (inducements), Bloch (expression through materials), Joyce (digital resistance), Burrowes (creative and disruptive intervention) and refines them with new contributions to present an updated universal typology of civil resistance tactics.

CHAPTER 4. Mapping New Civil Resistance Tactics

In this monograph, we categorize civil resistance tactics into three major categories: saying, not doing, and doing.

Saying: Also called acts of expression

- Protest and appeal: What we say, or how we say things

Not doing: Also called acts of omission

- Noncooperation and refraining: What we don't do, or how we don't do things

Doing: Also called acts of commission

- Disruptive intervention: What we do or how we disrupt things
- Creative intervention: What we make or how we create things

Saying (acts of expression) includes protesting through communication such as yelling and chanting, as well as persuasive communication forms such as humor and prayers. Most acts of expression can be used to penalize or reward, so in this monograph we follow Gene Sharp's methodology of grouping expressive methods together in a category called protest and appeal.

Not doing (acts of omission) includes noncooperation (not doing something that adversaries want you to do) and a new category for the constructive technique we call refraining (halting something that adversaries don't want you to do). The acts of omission category can be misleading in implying passivity or that no action is involved. However, most strikes and boycotts are very active. Sharp's use of the infinitive "to withdraw cooperation" as a description of noncooperation methods highlights the active dimension of these tactics. Refraining tactics as part of the acts of omission category may include the suspension of a labor strike or the halt of disruptive actions that inflict costs on one's adversary. It is often used as a positive incentive that is unilaterally initiated by the movement, though does not include actions taken as a result of a negotiated agreement between a movement and its opponent.

Doing or creating (acts of commission) includes disruptive intervention and creative intervention. Examples of disruptive intervention include blockades, phone jamming, and sit-ins. Creative interventions construct and model the society that activists seek to create. Sharp correctly points out that the latter methods "establish new political and social patterns and behaviors," but he does not classify them separately from methods that "disrupt... established behavior patterns" of adversaries. Bartkowski (2013) and Dudouet (2014) label these tactics as "creative nonviolent interventions." They encompass some elements called constructive programs and pre-figurative actions such as mock elections, parallel governments, and alternative schools. Creative intervention also includes what Vinthagen calls "utopian enactments" such as new social behaviors or institutions that prefigure the world that proponents want to create. It could also involve taking over and operating the other party's existing institutions such as a police station, checkpoint, or factory.

All civil resistance tactics are a form of communication in a social environment. Acts of saying, specifically, are often used similarly to a "propaganda of the deed" to inspire a revolt by demonstrating that the opponent's control was indeed not total and that ordinary people had both the will and space to rebel. Acts of saying include communication through direct action, as made famous by the Industrial Workers of the World (IWW or Wobblies)—the labor activists who engaged in many intense labor strikes in the early 20th century to communicate their opposition to the owning class. Acts of not doing are powerful weapons of nonviolent coercion or pressure on the opponent while acts of doing or creating are primarily used to control resources and/or usurp power, often through engagement (intervention) in alternative practices, parallel institutions, and self-organizing.

Table 4 incorporates the framework introduced in Table 1 to map corresponding new tactics of civil resistance. Only one new tactic was assigned for each major category (in total, 23 tactics), though many more new tactics have been identified in the Universe of Nonviolent Tactics Appendix and in the Nonviolent Tactics Database.

TABLE 4: Mapping New Civil Resistance Tactics

Resistance behavior	NATURE OF TACTIC INDUCEMENTS — CONFRONTATIONAL (COERCIVE)				
	Protest — Communicative action to criticize or coerce				
Saying (acts of expression)	HUMAN BODY **Flash mob**	MATERIAL ARTS ***Cacerolazo***	DIGITAL TECHNOLOGY **Digital game**	HUMAN LANGUAGE **Mic check**	
	Noncooperation — Refusal to engage in expected behavior through boycotts and strikes in order to penalize or increase costs on the opponent				
Not doing (acts of omission)	POLITICAL **Inter-agency noncooperation**	SOCIAL **Withholding religious rites**	ECONOMIC **Divestment**		
	Disruptive Intervention — Direct action that confronts another party to stop, disrupt, or change their behavior				
Doing or creating something (acts of commission)	POLITICAL/JUDICIAL **Parliamentary disruption**	ECONOMIC **Business whistle-blowing**	SOCIAL **Outing**	PHYSICAL **Die-in**	PSYCHOLOGICAL **Self-mutilation**

Mapping New Civil Resistance Tactics, cont.

NATURE OF TACTIC INDUCEMENTS					Resistance behavior
CONSTRUCTIVE (PERSUASIVE)					
Appeal — Communicative actions to inform or persuade					
HUMAN BODY **Growing hair**	MATERIAL ARTS **Murals**	DIGITAL TECHNOLOGY **Sousveillance**		HUMAN LANGUAGE **Public advertisement**	**Saying** (acts of expression)
Refraining — Halting or calling off a planned or ongoing action to reward or persuade the opponent					
	SUSPENDING **Suspending an ongoing nonviolent disruptive action**	ACTIVE ABSTENTION **Active abstention from a planned nonviolent action**			**Not doing** (acts of omission)
Creative Intervention — Direct action that models or constructs alternative (competing) behaviors and institutions or takes over existing institutions					
POLITICAL/JUDICIAL **Citizen inspections**	ECONOMIC **Property expropriation**	SOCIAL **Marriage inclusion**	PHYSICAL **Critical mass**	PSYCHOLOGICAL **Self-imposed transparency**	**Doing or creating something** (acts of commission)

CHAPTER 5. New Civil Resistance Tactics: Selection Criteria, Descriptions, and Examples

The Criteria for Selecting New Civil Resistance Tactics

This monograph uses specific criteria to identify new civil resistance tactics along the lines of Gene Sharp's previous efforts. Consequently, to be included in this monograph's categorization, the new civil resistance tactics must:

A. coerce or persuade a group or society to change the status quo they support (a governing system, a policy or practice, etc.) in a contentious conflict

B. not physically threaten or injure others or most kinds of property

C. not be routine or institutional processes with known procedural outcomes such as laws, courts, elections, lobbying, and commerce

D. be plausibly replicable in a variety of conflicts or contexts

E. not be an action by a non-partisan third-party (external) actor such as nonviolent civilian protection activities

F. be unilateral and not require the cooperation of an adversary

G. not be primarily logistical campaign activities such as training and fundraising

The above criteria were used to identify hundreds of new tactics listed in the Universe of Nonviolent Tactics Appendix. Below is a sampling of the newly identified tactics in the new proposed categorization. Many tactics, as Sharp wrote, can fit into more than one category based on function or, in some cases, intended impact.

The tactics are divided into broad categories of resistance behaviors such as saying (acts of expression), not doing something (acts of omission), and doing or creating something (acts of commission). We also divide methods according to whether they are confrontational and coercive, or constructive and persuasive. Many new tactics beyond the ones described below have been identified for each of the categories and their full list is provided in the Universe of Nonviolent Tactics Appendix and described in the Nonviolent Tactics Database.

In this chapter, we offer a couple of examples of new tactics falling into each category or subcategory to highlight tactics not included in Sharp's list of 198 nonviolent methods.

Tactics of "Saying" Something (Protest and Appeal)

Resistance behavior	NATURE OF TACTIC INDUCEMENTS							
	CONFRONTATIONAL (COERCIVE)				CONSTRUCTIVE (PERSUASIVE)			
	Protest Communicative action to criticize or coerce				Appeal Communicative actions to inform or persuade			
Saying (acts of expression)	HUMAN BODY	MATERIAL ARTS	DIGITAL TECHNOLOGY	HUMAN LANGUAGE	HUMAN BODY	MATERIAL ARTS	DIGITAL TECHNOLOGY	HUMAN LANGUAGE
	Flash mob	Cacerolazo	Digital game	Mic check	Growing hair	Murals	Sousveillance	Public advertisement

This broad category includes verbal, linguistic, behavioral, and visual expressions of positive appeals and negative criticisms. All actions in society—including occupations and fair-trade markets—are a form of communication. However, this category of tactics is designated for actions whose purpose is primarily and commonly seen as communicative. Expressive tactics can be used for confrontation and threats (protest) as well as for constructive expressions or offers (appeal); their categorization in negative or positive boxes is fairly arbitrary and highly contextual.

We organize expressive methods into four sub-categories based on the primary medium in which they are conducted:

A. Human body;

B. Material arts;

C. Digital/Internet technology; and

D. Human language.

The following sections provide two examples of tactics for each of the aforementioned subcategories.

■ Human Body as the Primary Medium of Expression

FLASH MOBS (PROTEST)

Flash mobs are gatherings of people, usually recorded on digital media, performing actions such as street theater, a sit-down protest, or a blockade, at a specific time and place unbeknownst to the public ahead of time. A flash mob is typically performed in a busy area where it will be heavily witnessed, such as a train station, a park square, or the middle of a college campus. It can be an unrehearsed action that observers can join.

Flash mobs began as a form of participatory art and has evolved into a mechanism of political protest. One political example of this tactic is a 2009 flash mob in which hundreds of protesters dressed in business attire stormed Wall Street and took part in a mass pillow fight to "demand their bailouts." In Thailand, Belarus, and Zimbabwe, protesters have used flash mobs to show outrage over laws banning protests or public gatherings. In Thailand specifically, flash mobs were used in 2014 as a means to quickly disperse and reorganize in the event of police repression. In contrast to Thailand, security forces in Belarus arrested protesters during a flash mob in which participants simply clapped their hands. The absurd images of brutal arrests in response to clapping helped bolster anti-Lukashenko sentiment in Belarus (Mitchell and Boyd 2012).

GROWING HAIR (APPEAL)

Growing hair was a cultural tactic in many Western nations in the 1960s and 70s. It was part of a generational effort to challenge societal assumptions and norms. Growing long hair was about making a "back to the land" and "natural" statement and was associated around the world with anti-war movements. Feminists stopped shaving underarm and leg hair in efforts to challenge different gender grooming standards in society. Growing beards has also been utilized as a form of protest. In 1981, New York City police officers grew beards during stalled contract talks.

■ Material Art as the Primary Media of Expression

These tactics use material objects, sound, and light including puppets, banners, colored clothing, flags, food, music, and headlights. Art has been at the forefront of many nonviolent campaigns serving the purpose of both protest and appeal (Bloch, 2015). Two examples not included in Sharp's classic list include:

CACEROLAZO (PROTEST)

Invented in the 1970s, *cacerolazo* is a much louder form of protesting than most. Participants bring metal cookware into the streets to bang them noisily. In a poignant 2016 example, Venezuelan protesters reintroduced *cacerolazos* as a way to express their frustrations with President Nicolás Maduro. They protested the state of the economy—which for many meant lack of food—making the symbolism of the using pots as protest props all the more meaningful. Some *cacerolazo* actions have been conducted from numerous homes simultaneously to limit police retaliations. Women have historically participated in *cacerolazos* in large numbers. To sustain noise levels and to prevent headaches, earplugs are commonly used by those participating (Ulmer, 2016; Christoff).

MURALS (APPEAL)

Murals use material arts in a way that is constructive and persuasive, attempting to inspire an audience. Murals are large-scale paintings on the sides of buildings or walls. During the dictatorship of General Pinochet in Chile, photographer Andrés Romero Spethman followed multiple mural brigades that drew vivid depictions of the social and political issues in the country. The murals, often covering entire walls, featured satirical representations of political figures and images of hope for the Chilean people. Soon after their completion, however, the government removed them (Harvard Digital Collection, n.d.).

Murals have been deployed in conflicts across the globe, from East Timor to Palestine to Northern Ireland. In the 2007 Face 2 Face project, Palestinians and Israelis were photographed engaging in the same work, and their portraits were glued to the separation wall in cities on both sides of the wall. A variation of this project is the creation of "sister murals." For example, the creation of twin murals was coordinated between Olympia, Washington (USA) and Rafah in the Gaza Strip to raise awareness and solidarity. Unfortunately, mural projects are susceptible to "redecoration" and modification by others. For example, after the fall of Egyptian President Hosni Mubarak, competing political groups added many layers of murals over those made in Tahrir Square.[43]

■ Digital/Internet Technology as the Primary Medium of Expression

The digital revolution, both as a communication delivery device and an environment for engaging in power struggle and conflict, has led to the formation and emergence of new civil resistance methods. Most of these methods fall into the appeal and protest category and their development has been closely tracked by the work of Dr. Mary Joyce and colleagues in Civil Resistance 2.0, cited earlier in this monograph. Most digital methods can be used for protest and/or appeal. Here are two examples:

DIGITAL GAMES (PROTEST)

Digital games have been used to strengthen public opposition for a political cause. In Mexico, programmers developed an online game to criticize the values of Donald Trump, who was at the time a U.S. presidential candidate. The game consists of users playing the role of Donald Trump, trying to collect as much money as possible, marginalizing minorities, and whipping his hair around (Matthews, 2015). In 2019, protesters in Hong Kong developed an interactive, virtual reality-based video game to show players what it is like to protest on the streets. The game allows players to learn about important events which have occurred during the movement, and to perform maneuvers such as dodging tear gas or police. The game developers noted that the creation of the game was a form of protest in and of itself in the

---

43   Author observed this on a trip to Cairo in 2012.

wake of backlash from Google and Blizzard Entertainment, which had recently banned pro-Hong Kong players and games from their platforms (Reuters, 2019).

SOUSVEILLANCE (APPEAL)

Sousveillance, in contrast to surveillance, is when a participant in an activity records the activity. For example, in 2007, mobile phones were used in Sierra Leone and Ghana for investigating malpractice and intimidation during elections (Green, 2008). A subset of sousveillance is **inverse surveillance**, which typically involves the bottom-up surveillance of surveillance systems, institutions, and power structures. Examples of this range from privacy watch-dog groups to journalistic activities such as The Intercept's Secret Surveillance Catalogue, which logs the technologies that the U.S. government uses for surveillance. Activists commonly use sousveillance to deter police repression, even in cases where audio or video are not immediately broadcasted. Another subset is **alibi sousveillance**, in which individuals or groups record their activity as a way to defend against narrative manipulations. Nonviolent protesters may choose to live-stream their protest as a way to document their actions in case participants are arrested or falsely accused of wrong-doing.

■ Human Language as the Primary Medium of Expression

Some tactics focus on how humans express themselves through various languages. Several of these methods are described in terms of written media (newspapers, journals, books, etc.) which are manifested as methods when employed to protest or persuade in conflicts. Tactics using human language can make both appeals and threats in a variety of constructive and confrontational arenas.

HUMAN MICROPHONE OR MIC CHECK (PROTEST)

Popularized by the Occupy movement, the human microphone is a form of verbal communication utilized to help large audiences hear a speaker. Speakers deliver their message in short phrases and sentences which are immediately shouted by those within earshot and subsequently repeated two or three times by those standing farther away. The message travels throughout the crowd in a ripple effect, eventually reaching those who could not hear the speaker initially. It has the power to enable thousands of people to hear a speaker, in the absence of a microphone and sound system. This method can also help unify a crowd, improve communication and understanding, and have a powerful emotional impact on the speaker hearing one's words repeated by many others. It also tends to limit side conversations, which can help maintain a large crowd's attention and focus.

However, the process of repetitive shouting can be tiring. Secondary and tertiary repeats can become frayed and cacophonous, and the necessity of using short phrases can hinder the communication of complex thoughts. This method is increasingly being used as a form of protest to talk-over or interrupt speakers against whom campaigns are organizing, such as political candidates during election rallies (YouTube user "noplatform for IMF," 2013).

POLITICAL ADVERTISING (APPEAL)

Mainstream media continues to be a central platform for community and society conversations. A common tactic to inform or persuade as part of the human language subcategory of appeals is political advertising. Political advertising by corporations, political parties, and wealthy people is so routine in many countries that usually this would not be considered a nonviolent action tactic. However, when paid for by large numbers of individuals or groups who are commonly shut out of public discourse, paid political advertising is a means to publicize one's views and to advocate for different policies supported by a campaign or a movement. The targets of these messages can include movements' adversaries or the general readership and viewership of the media. Crowd-funded advertising has been run on TV, social media, billboards, newspapers, magazines, and radio. In 2015, Amnesty International crowd-funded from some 1,000 British citizens to pay for public advertisements to prevent the government from repealing human rights (Amnesty International UK, 2015).

Tactics of "Not Doing" (Noncooperation and Refraining)

Resistance behavior	NATURE OF TACTIC INDUCEMENTS				
	CONFRONTATIONAL (COERCIVE)			CONSTRUCTIVE (PERSUASIVE)	
Not doing (acts of omission)	**Noncooperation** — Refusal to engage in expected behavior through boycotts and strikes in order to penalize or increase costs on the opponent			**Refraining** — Halting or calling off a planned or ongoing action to reward or persuade the opponent	
	POLITICAL **Inter-agency noncooperation**	SOCIAL **Withholding religious rites**	ECONOMIC **Divestment**	SUSPENDING **Suspending an ongoing nonviolent disruptive action**	ACTIVE ABSTENTION **Active abstention from a planned nonviolent action**

Doing nothing is not usually seen as an act. But in the context of civil resistance, *intentionally* doing nothing in an environment where you are expected to do something is an act of omission. Tactics of omission can be divided into sub-categories called noncooperation and refraining.

Noncooperation is the refusal to engage in expected or required behavior. These tactics, that aim to withdraw cooperation from an adversary, constitute the vast majority of acts of omission. Sharp collected over 100 methods of noncooperation largely categorized into economic, social, or political spheres. This monograph maintains Sharp's subcategories of political, social, and economic noncooperation, while identifying new methods in each of these noncooperation subcategories.

In addition to noncooperation as a constructive act of omission, refraining involves halting or suspending noncooperation and disruptive actions or expressions in order to reward or persuade. Pioneered by Gandhi, these methods have not been categorized by analysts until now. These acts of omission are positive actions conducted unilaterally to communicate good-will to an adversary and/or the general public. They theoretically can be used to reward an opponent for good behavior, policies, or statements. They are a relatively rare practice.

Noncooperation Tactics: Confrontational Acts of Omission

The following sections provide two examples of tactics for each of the three subcategories: political noncooperation, economic noncooperation, and social noncooperation.

■ Political Noncooperation

Political noncooperation is an act of omission that involves withdrawing cooperation from political entities or requirements. Here is an example that is not included on Sharp's list of nonviolent action methods:

INTER-AGENCY NONCOOPERATION

Inter-agency noncooperation happens when a governmental or other agency withholds information or resources to prevent action, such as government repression of activists. During large protests in South Korea in 2015, the fire department turned off the water supply to fire hydrants so that the security forces could not water-hose protesters (Lee, 2016). Following an announcement from the US Immigration and Customs Enforcement agency (ICE) of planned mass raids to search for undocumented residents in major cities all across the country, several U.S. cities made declarations of noncooperation with the agency. The mayor of Chicago, Lori Lightfoot, ordered the city's police force not to cooperate with ICE and to cut off ICE's access to their database, specifically the information concerning immigration.

■ Social Noncooperation

Social noncooperation is an act of omission that involves refusing to engage in expected or required behavior in social and civil society settings. These methods are often categorized on a continuum of ostracization of individuals, noncooperation with specific events, customs, or institutions, and withdrawal from an entire social system.

WITHHOLDING OF RELIGIOUS RITES

Religious authorities may selectively withhold religious rites to worshippers who violate the teachings of the religious body or who are in conflict with the religious body. Interdicts and excommunications are additional methods of religious noncooperation that clergy use.

One example is Buddhist monks resisting Burmese generals in 1990 and in 2007. The monks turned over their alms bowls, refusing to accept food offerings from the military leaders who had assaulted monks and civilians. Buddhists believe that failure to provide food to monks will damage one's religious merit. Muslim clerics refused to cooperate with the Islamic State in France by refusing burial rites to a Muslim murderer of a Catholic priest (La Porte, 2016).

■ Economic Noncooperation

Economic noncooperation is an act of omission that involves refusing to sell one's labor (strike) or to buy a service or product (boycott).

DIVESTMENT

In the 1980s, major church denominations in the United States forced the seven major U.S. banks to divest their church pension investments from businesses profiting from apartheid in South Africa. Labor and national pension funds have also exerted influence by divesting from companies whose actions they oppose. Norway's Global Pension Fund of $900 billion divested from coal companies in 2015 to withdraw support from companies contributing to climate disruption (Crawford-Browne, 2017).

Refraining: Constructive Acts of Omission

Most examples of refraining are deployed as part of a constructive approach to conflict where those who use refraining want to persuade or appeal to an adversary or the public using an incentive of postponing or stopping a resistance action. While noncooperation is not doing what the opponents want you to do, refraining refers to not doing or doing more slowly what the opponent does not want you to do. This choice is strategic and deliberate, undertaken by activists to advance, not suspend, the struggle and to move closer to the realization of its goals. These methods are not a result of backing down or giving up. Refraining can also be understood as a form of voluntary cooperation to reward an adversary or the general public in the short term, in order to change the dynamics of the struggle to help achieve campaign goals in the long term.

Refraining methods intentionally stop or suspend an ongoing action or prevent a planned action. They should not be confused with suspensions or collapses of strikes, blockades, or occupations as a result of campaign failures. Clever strategists undoubtedly seek to re-frame their retreats (refraining) in positive terms in order to re-group and fight another day. The purpose of these tactics can also aim to unify or strengthen the will of the campaigners.

Refraining tactics, like most constructive methods of action, entail risk, particularly strategic risk. The opponents or adversaries may not react positively to rewards or incentives. They may question the sincerity or motivations of the nonviolent actors. An opponent might also misinterpret these methods as a sign of movement weakness and, instead of agreeing to negotiate, take the opportunity to instigate more violence. Thus, lessening pressure on an adversary could incite stronger attacks. Still, such tactics can be used effectively.

Refraining has no subcategories. Instead, we have identified two kinds of tactics: actions that aim to cease or freeze an ongoing tactic (**suspending**) and actions that prevent a planned action from taking place (**active abstention**). Here are two examples of refraining tactics:

■ Suspending

An act of omission in which one temporarily stops an ongoing action that the opponent opposes.

SUSPENDING AN ONGOING NONVIOLENT DISRUPTIVE ACTION

In 2017, airport workers in Newark, New Jersey (USA) unilaterally suspended their strike against unfair labor practices as a goodwill gesture to the public and the authorities (News12, 2017). The strike began when the airlines rejected the workers' attempts to organize a union and negotiate better hours and pay. The strike was suspended when American Airlines finally agreed to meet with their union representative. The airport went on to recognize the union and since then mutual cooperation has continued.

■ Active Abstention

An act that prevents a planned action against the opponent from taking place.

ACTIVE ABSTENTION FROM A PLANNED NONVIOLENT ACTION

On March 30, 1981, the Solidarity trade union in Poland planned a general strike to protest police brutality against workers. Movement leader Lech Wałęsa unilaterally called off the general strike after the Communist government agreed to negotiate and offered concessions.

Tactics of "Doing or Creating" Something (Disruptive and Creative Interventions)

Resistance behavior	NATURE OF TACTIC INDUCEMENTS									
	CONFRONTATIONAL (COERCIVE)					CONSTRUCTIVE (PERSUASIVE)				
	Disruptive Intervention Direct action that confronts another party to stop, disrupt, or change their behavior					**Creative Intervention** Direct action that models or constructs alternative (competing) behaviors and institutions or takes over existing institutions				
Doing or creating something (acts of commission)	POLITICAL/ JUDICIAL	ECONOMIC	SOCIAL	PHYSICAL	PSYCHO-LOGICAL	POLITICAL/ JUDICIAL	ECONOMIC	SOCIAL	PHYSICAL	PSYCHO-LOGICAL
	Parliamentary disruption	Business whistle-blowing	Outing	Die-in	Self-mutilation	Citizen inspections	Property expropriation	Marriage inclusion	Critical mass	Self-imposed transparency

This monograph divides Sharp's large category of intervention methods into creative and disruptive interventions. Disruptive interventions are direct actions with the purpose of pressuring another party to stop, disrupt, or change its behavior. This category of methods seeks to "step more directly in between the adversary and the achievement of its purpose" (McCarthy 1997, 323). Traditional examples include blockades, invasions, hunger strikes, and denial of service. A few everyday resistance tactics are included such as counterfeiting and desertion.

Creative interventions are direct actions that prefigure (model or construct) alternative behaviors, norms, and institutions. Common examples include parallel government, alternative currency, alternative newspapers, or alternative language. Also included are rare interventions of unilateral rewards or offers, as well as elements of constructive programs that don't just strengthen internal campaigns but have elements that disrupt or challenge an adversary's interests. A few everyday resistance tactics are included such as black markets. This monograph maintains Sharp's subcategories for methods of intervention (political, economic, social, physical, and psychological), and identifies and adds new tactics for each of these sub-categories.

Disruptive Interventions: Confrontational Acts of Commission

The following sections provide one example of tactics for each of the five subcategories of disruptive interventions: political, economic, social, physical, and psychological.

■ Political/Judicial Disruptive Intervention

An act of commission, this intervention is used in political and judicial arenas to obstruct or subvert an opponent's government or legal system.

PARLIAMENTARY/LEGISLATURE/COUNCIL DISRUPTION

This method is conducted by legislators who stop or slow down legislative proceedings by extra-legal or extra-regulatory means. Disruption often happens through shouting, singing, or chanting. Sit-ins and other physically disruptive actions are also deployed, usually to stop votes. Tools or instruments used in parliamentary proceedings can also be taken away, such as a symbolic mace in Nigeria that was removed to prevent parliament from passing laws until it was returned (Taylor, 2018). Another example of legislative disruption was in July 2018, when members of the European Parliament turned off their microphones in support of striking interpreters (France24, 2018).

■ Economic Disruptive Intervention

This tactical intervention occurs in the economic sphere and is primarily focused on imposing financial costs upon an opponent.

BUSINESS WHISTLEBLOWING

Whistleblowing refers to when journalists or insiders release information. A whistleblower is anyone who reports insider knowledge of illegal activities occurring in a business, including employees, contractors, suppliers, or clients. Whistleblowers can become aware of the illegal activity by directly witnessing the behavior, reading insider information, or being told about it. An insider who leaks information secretly or confidentially to a journalist or other whistleblower is referred to as a leaker. Businesses around the world have been exposed and held accountable by insiders who provided information on dangerous practices.

One example is a Russian auditor named Sergei Magnitsky who blew the whistle on Russian police who had given confiscated materials to criminals (high-ranking Russian officials and Kremlin-connected businessmen), who then used the information obtained from the materials to take over three Hermitage companies and fraudulently reclaim $230 million of the taxes previously paid by Hermitage (Browder, 2015).

Whistleblowing is typically seen as an act of betrayal by the affected institution, and retribution and suppression can be severe. As a result of his whistleblowing, Magnitsky was tortured and beaten to death by police in prison. It can be a high-risk but high-impact tactic and should be considered carefully.

■ Social Disruptive Intervention

This type of tactical intervention "takes the form of direct intrusion in social behavior patterns, social occasions, and social institutions" (Sharp, 1973).

OUTING

This is a technique of revealing a secret about someone's personal life that conflicts with their political or public actions. In the 1980s, members of the gay community exposed politicians' homosexual behavior to demonstrate a contradiction with their public condemnation of homosexuality or support for laws and norms that repressed the gay community. Another example of outing is male politicians being exposed for encouraging their impregnated partner to seek abortions while publicly advocating to ban the procedure. Such exposure is typically done through the arts or reputable news organizations but can also be done through social media or law enforcement.

■ Physical Disruptive Intervention

This type of tactical intervention consists of deploying bodies or things in places where they are not legal or wanted, in order to obstruct, disrupt, or interfere with an opponent or their allies.

DIE-IN

Also known as a lie-in, this technique involves protesters simulating being dead as a strategy for occupying a space. Die-ins are often not simply a theatrical production. The point is to block foot or vehicle traffic and attract attention, so participants will often cover themselves with signs, fake blood, or other props. Though die-ins can be traced back over 50 years, in the last decade they have increased in popularity. In 2016, activists in Hong Kong protested the mass killing of sharks for soup by engaging in a die-in dressed in bloody shark suits (Efe, 2016). The use of blood or fake blood is common, as well as drawing chalk outlines of bodies that remain long after the protest has ended.

■ Psychological Disruptive Intervention

This type of tactic is a highly contentious form of intervention as it can be implemented through self-suffering or dramatization meant to force attention to one's message or needs.

SELF-MUTILATION (OR BODY ART)

This is a technique of self-sacrifice and often cultural transgression which seeks to disrupt the narrative of an opponent or society. A common form of self-mutilation is sewing one's lips shut to dramatize a cause with the visual statement of being silenced or censored and/or as a way to amplify a fast. Refugees stranded in prisons or camps have engaged in this practice in many countries. Tattoos are another common way to promote one's views. Animal rights activists have branded themselves with hot irons to demonstrate the cruelty of branding animals. Shaving one's head can be a temporary form of bodily mutilation since hair typically grows back.

Self-mutilation is understood as some form of self-harm without suicidal intent. Some argue that self-mutilation falls into the category of nonviolent action because no one, other than the actionist, is harmed. Others argue that a method can only fall under the category of nonviolent action if it does not cause harm to anyone, including the actionist.

Creative Intervention: Constructive Acts of Commission

As noted above, this monograph introduces a self-standing category of nonviolent tactics: creative intervention (also known as prefigurative methods or constructive program). These tactics include efforts to establish patterns of behavior and norms or political, economic, social, and cultural institutions that in some way challenge the established order or an adversary. These actions sometimes use rewards and constructive approaches to persuade and/or lessen the defensiveness of an opponent or an opponent's control over society—without necessarily challenging them directly. This intervention often aims at a long-term transformation of society, rather than immediately targeting a visible opponent (e.g., head of a regime). Common tactics include alternative markets, transportation systems, social institutions, communications, economic institutions, and dual sovereignty and parallel government.

American settlers in the 18th century, Poles and Algerians in the 19th century, and Ghanaians and Zambians in the 20th century built indigenous economic, social, political, and religious associations as a form of resistance against colonization—often parallel to the formal institutions of the subjugating system. Gandhi helped popularize relentless action as a form of cultural and economic resistance. He famously led Indians to spin cotton to encourage self-reliance and to decrease dependency on the British textile mills. The spinning wheel remains the central motif on the national flag of India. Gandhi also famously walked to the sea and encouraged others to make their own salt (an illegal activity), which he believed was the right of any Indian. Millions of Indians joined him, and the British colonial regime was shaken and weakened due to the loss of tax revenue and the practice of massive disobedience. The constructive intervention used in a conflictual setting has various names including prefigurative action, constructive program, creative intervention, institution building, parallel institutions, cultural resistance, acting-out-the-future-today, and nonviolent action to "make or create."

The reverse strike produces an unusual example of unilaterally rewarding an opponent, such as in Italy when unemployed men (that the government was not helping) repaired a much-needed road (that the government was not repairing).

Here are some newly identified tactics for each of the five subcategories of creative interventions: political, economic, social, physical, and psychological.

■ Political/Judicial Creative Intervention

This intervention is a positive set of physical and material actions that seek to reward or persuade an opponent or potential ally to tolerate or support a movement's goals. Examples include reverse trials, mock elections, and citizen inspections.

CITIZEN INSPECTIONS

Citizens inspect the work of government officials to obtain and release data that compromise the agency and draw support for a movement's cause. In the 1970s in Pennsylvania (USA), a citizen inspection team secretly "inspected" an FBI field office and removed documents that proved massive illegal surveillance and sabotage against social movements on the part of the FBI. While not directly advocating for replicated citizen inspections, this effort succeeded in pressuring lawmakers to engage in stronger oversight and to curtail abuses by unaccountable law enforcement agencies. Another example comes from East German citizens who entered the Secret Police's main headquarters in East Berlin on January 15, 1990, and saved important, revelatory files from planned destruction. Other citizen investigators uncovered Secret Police surveillance equipment in businesses and the post office in the East German capital.

However, citizen inspections are sometimes theatrical productions that feature large magnifying glasses and cameras because authorities often deny physical entry to a space.

■ Economic Creative Intervention

These tactics seek to establish new economic institutions or relationships through a reward system to persuade an opponent or to model better ways of organizing economic affairs. Examples of this include buycotts (e.g., buying services or products from others instead of from boycotted opponents), copyleft (alternative to copyright, making materials freely available as long as attributions are provided), and property expropriation (the latter explained below).

PROPERTY EXPROPRIATION

This tactic involves workers permanently taking over factories and turning them into cooperative worker-owned enterprises. In 2001, more than 300 factories were bankrupted in the economic collapse in Argentina. Bankrupt owners fled because of charges of fraud or they were simply replaced by the workers who took over management and ownership of the enterprises (Balch, 2013).

Property expropriation is an example of a powerful kind of nonviolent action that is best expressed by the term "takeover." There are many instances in which an abusive state (or in this case, corporations) is confronted by mass actions in which state institutions are not replaced with new ones, but are simply taken over and the old employees pushed out. These methods do not always fit comfortably in our category of persuasive or reward actions.

■ Social Creative Intervention

An act of commission, this category of action is defined by physical or material actions to change social behaviors and cultural institutions in constructive ways. In self-determination and identity conflicts, activists sometimes use these methods in conjunction with political and economic objectives. Examples of this include women becoming religious leaders without official approval, pray-ins, and marriage inclusion (the latter explained below).

MARRIAGE INCLUSION

Marriage is a global cultural practice strongly tied to religion. Throughout history, there have been many transgressive examples of people seeking to marry despite social, religious, or legal taboos. When many people seek to celebrate taboo marriage in a coordinated effort, it constitutes civil resistance. One recent example is the same-sex marriage equality movement. Beginning in the 1970s, same-sex couples began openly participating in alternative marriage ceremonies in various European and North American countries. These marriages were not legally recognized by any jurisdiction.

In many countries, religious institutions conduct marriages which are then ratified by the state. LGBTQ activists began campaigns to persuade their religious communities to conduct their marriages, even if the state refused to recognize them. The LGBTQ community, excluded from most religious communities, organized its own church called the Metropolitan Community Church (MCC). The MCC has grown to over 220 congregations (as of 2017),[44] some of which are still operating illegally in countries such as Uganda, Nigeria, Iran, and Saudi Arabia, where members face extreme risk. The MCC conducted its first marriage in 1969. Subsequently, in the 1970s, various denominations began performing same-sex unions and, by the 1990s, same-sex marriages. Although not then recognized by law, these denominations helped apply political, moral, and social pressure on the public, the legal system, and legislators to support same-sex marriage.

---

44 For more information, see **https://www.mccchurch.org/**.

■ Physical Creative Intervention

These methods primarily use human bodies or materials to obstruct the opponent by means of new social practices or material changes, such as digging up tarmac to create a garden. Examples of this include kiss-ins, defiance of blockades, and critical mass (the latter explained below).

CRITICAL MASS (CYCLING)

Cyclists organize critical mass actions regularly in an effort to reclaim the streets from motor vehicles. In these protests, cyclists gather in large numbers—typically on the afternoon of the last Friday of the month—and hold a mass improvisational ride through city streets, often disobeying traffic laws. This event originated in its modern form in 1992 in San Francisco, California (USA) (Garofoli, 2002). The purposes of the event included challenging the domination of motor vehicles, encouraging respect for cyclists, and modeling a future in which cycling is the dominant (more environmentally friendly) form of transportation.

■ Psychological Creative Intervention

These methods focus on psychology, using rewards or new paradigms to influence how people think. Examples include awards as encouragement, flowers in guns, and self-imposed transparency (the latter explained below).

SELF-IMPOSED TRANSPARENCY

A major challenge for organizers of the 2012 protests against rigged parliamentary elections in Russia was to convince potential protesters to trust the organizers. In an effort to do so, the Networked Public TV (SOTV), a new online channel, broadcast discussions about the behind-the-scenes of organizing protests, including the financials. Voluntary financial transparency is thus a powerful technique, not only to increase organizers' credibility, but also to shame an opaque and corrupt government.

The 23 tactics described above are a sampling of a large and growing dataset in the field of civil resistance. The tactics vary widely in location, cultural or political contexts, size, and frequency. Some tactics also overlap in terms of their persuasive or coercive character. Many tactics also fall on the margins of civil resistance movements, which will be discussed in the next chapter.

CHAPTER 6. On the Edges of Civil Resistance Tactics

On the edges of mass political action are tactics that were excluded purposefully from the list of nonviolent methods compiled in the Universe of Nonviolent Tactics Appendix. Some of them are routine (an everyday behavior), yet they might still create a pattern of nonviolent subversion and resistance. Others are violent, though might be used within nonviolent campaigns and perceived by some to be nonviolent and/or justified because they do not physically harm others. Given the ongoing debates around these actions and their frequent entanglement with civil resistance, they are identified with brief elaborations below.

Everyday Resistance

Everyday resistance, according to Scott (2008, 21), is criticized for its inclusion as a civil resistance phenomenon because these actions: "1) [are] unorganized, unsystematic, and individual; 2) [are] opportunistic and self-indulgent; 3) [have] no revolutionary consequences; and/or 4) imply in their intention or logic an accommodation with the structure of domination." As a result of these characteristics, everyday resistance has remained outside of some civil resistance scholars' purview.

Certainly, challenging the status quo by breaking established norms and disruption is at the heart of most nonviolent civil resistance. But civil resistance organizers would consider many of the norm or law-breaking instances of everyday resistance, such as stealing and lying, as common criminality or examples of means that do not match the ends and, thus, fall outside of the nonviolent resistance repertoire.

The term "everyday resistance" can cause confusion with the daily resistance of the constructive program. Both are actions that occur on a continual basis such as spinning cotton, attending a language school for an unrecognized minority language, squatting, tax evasion, or creating autonomous social space for the assertion of dignity. One distinction between many of these actions is that many constructive programs are visible and many everyday resistance activities are disguised.

Property Destruction and Transformation

Many movements frequently use property destruction and transformation (both being recognizably subjective terms). Sharp and many practitioners exclude this type of action from the nonviolent method repertoire. Some campaigns focus on property transformation as constructive program rather than a nonviolent sanction. The Christian anti-nuclear weapons group, Plowshares, physically hammers on nuclear weapons delivery systems and their infrastructure. Plowshare activists, acting out the Bible's verse on beating swords into plowshares, seek to transform nuclear weapons and their delivery systems into allegorical plowshares.

Environmental activists have burned, destroyed, and damaged property such as animal cages, dams, fur coats, and ski lodges. Many countries have experienced campaigns in which citizens transcribed or stamped money with protest messages. Anarchists, suffragettes, and others have engaged in attacks on private and corporate property as a form of protest.

If an artist joined a campaign and sacrificed their own painting as a tactic, we would consider their destruction of their own property to be a method of nonviolent action. On the other hand, when José Bové, a French farmer, smashed a McDonald's restaurant with a tractor, it may have been justified, but it is not considered nonviolent action. Destruction of communal or public property is highly contextual but, generally speaking, it is excluded from our definition of nonviolent action.

Some argue that property destruction can be considered nonviolent action if no person is physically targeted or hurt. However, no one considers the burning of the Reichstag (Germany's Parliament) in 1933 to be a nonviolent action. Many believe that most forms of property destruction are akin to a physical threat or violence. Marxists and anarchists, among others, critique the private ownership of the means of production as a form of profound oppression of the 99%. As a result, for-profit corporations, particularly banks, have been regularly targeted with window smashing.

Since the labeling of property destruction tactics as violent or nonviolent is so contextual, many have focused their attention on the effectiveness of property destruction in a nonviolent campaign. Tom Hastings has proposed a list of five elements that determine whether the destruction of something may be helpful to a nonviolent campaign, including the premise "that no private individual's property is destroyed" (Hastings, 2020).[45]

These acts have been controversial in terms of morality and effectiveness. Some activists believe that public property destruction is ineffective and counterproductive because it can cause opponents to harden their stance and steer potential allies away from sympathizing with and supporting the destructive group. Property destruction and transformation tactics are used (often controversially) in nonviolent civil resistance. Advice on strategies for effectively using property destruction are beyond the scope of this study.

---

45 For more information, see: Hastings, Tom. "Property Damage, Violence, Nonviolent Action, and Strategy." *Minds of the Movement* (blog). ICNC, June 2, 2020. **https://www.nonviolent-conflict.org/blog_post/property-damage-violence-nonviolent-action-and-strategy/**.

Suicide

Activist suicides are another method that is sometimes utilized in nonviolent campaigns. These activists have sacrificed their lives without threatening or injuring their opponents. Irish nationalist Bobby Sands fasted to death in British prisons while demanding British expulsion from Northern Ireland. A Korean farmer killed himself standing on top of police barricades in Mexico during protests against the World Trade Organization's policies. Self-immolation has also been widely used in movements around the world. Examples include Tibetans protesting Chinese occupation, Vietnamese and Americans protesting U.S. occupation of Vietnam, and a Pole in 2017 protesting the conservative government that he saw as a threat to democracy.

In addition, thousands of citizens have died by exposing themselves to high-risk situations such as Rachel Corrie who, on March 16, 2003, stood in front of an Israeli bulldozer in Palestine. In 1913, suffragette Emily Davison died attempting to hang a banner while riding a galloping horse in front of the British King. In India, the Iron Lady of Manipur tried to kill herself in a 16-year long hunger strike (2000 to 2016) against police violence and impunity. She was arrested and force-fed regularly by the Indian military.

Suicide is widely perceived as a violent and psychologically brutal act, particularly when done without the support of fellow campaigners and/or family. Groups or campaigns have organized very few suicidal acts, and these are therefore considered renegade actions.

However, the right-to-die movement may be an exception. Within this movement, individuals with limited time to live and poor quality of life are committing suicide with the planned support of their friends and, in some cases, physicians. Civil disobedience against laws forbidding suicide for terminally ill patients is a world-wide phenomenon. Bond et al. describe suicide as a violent practice with a high level of contentiousness and almost no coercive component, instead relying on altruist appeals of empathy to pressure for change. Further study is needed on the effectiveness of suicide as a method of civil resistance in various contexts. Suicidal actions are excluded from the list of nonviolent methods listed in the Universe of Nonviolent Tactics Appendix.

Third-Party Nonviolent Actions

Mohandas Gandhi proposed the *Shanti Sena* (a peace army) as a third-party to intervene nonviolently in sectarian conflict. Beginning in the early 1980s, this inspired groups such as Peace Brigades International and Witness for Peace to send individuals to Central America to protect citizens from harm at the hands of the state and other armed actors. Using their privilege to monitor without becoming solidarity activists, these individuals developed a set of nonviolent techniques to protect civilians that has now been taken up by many other groups around the world.

Examples of non-partisan methods include accompaniment of threatened human rights defenders, protective presence for indigenous people or groups, reporting threats and humanizing actors, and witnessing. Mahoney and Eguren (1997), Schweitzer (2001, 2010), and Clark (2009) have documented and analyzed the emergence of non-partisan third-party action.[46] Civil resisters have appropriated some of these techniques and applied them in their grassroots campaigns for social change. For example, in Colombia, locals (who have some political or social status) have accompanied human rights defenders to provide security—something that was previously only carried out by non-partisan foreigners.

The boundaries of partisanship and parties in a conflict vary. The International Solidarity Movement and Christian Peacemaker Teams use some of these techniques in Palestine and elsewhere as invited outsiders with a solidarity viewpoint. In some cases, these groups become direct participants in the conflict and these non-partisan techniques (such as reporting) could be considered methods of civil resistance. Foreigners who are seen as actively intervening on behalf of one side of a conflict are often deported or denied visas, and therefore solidarity activists sometimes cannot sustain the techniques. Most third-party nonviolent interventions are not currently included in the Universe of Nonviolent Tactics Appendix, unless local actors have appropriated the intervention, as is sometimes the case with internal accompaniment led by movement members or their supporters.

Negotiation and Dialogue

Negotiation in the context of civil resistance campaigns is often thought of as a dialogue across a negotiating table at a point in a conflict when the parties believe it useful or necessary to reach an agreement. Wanis-St. John and Rosen (2017) propose a close relationship between successful negotiation and civil resistance in which civil resisters generate leverage

---

[46] Beer (1995) presented 11 types of third-party nonviolent interventions (TPNI): accompaniment, delegations, economic sanctions such as boycotts, election monitoring, human rights observation and investigations, information gathering and polling, media, mediation, peace walks/boating, physical interposition, and rescue teams/humanitarian assistance. Hunter and Lakey (2003) have identified four types of TPNI: interposition, observing/monitoring, protective accompaniment, and presence. Burrowes (Moser-Puangsuwan and Weber, 2000) classifies cross-border action on behalf of indigenous nonviolent movements across nine categories: local nonviolent campaigns, mobilization actions, nonviolent humanitarian assistance, nonviolent witness and accompaniment, nonviolent intercession, nonviolent solidarity, and nonviolent reconciliation and development. Dudouet (2015) defines nonviolent intervention by focusing on relational mechanisms vis-à-vis local campaigners or power-holders: promoting, capacity-building, connecting, protecting, monitoring, and pressuring.

for negotiators, who in return obtain benefits from an adversary.[47] Negotiations have not typically been included as a tactic of nonviolent action because they are not unilaterally initiated; they require an interlocutor. In addition, classic negotiations have procedurally known outcomes: a) agreements are reached, or b) agreements are not reached. Dialogue likewise is not considered a civil resistance tactic here because it requires the participation of an adversary. There are, however, numerous examples of dialogues that take the form of civil disobedience because they are forbidden.

Wanis-St. John writes that the "symbiosis between civil resistance and negotiation is long-standing. Martin Luther King Jr.'s logic was to compel segregationists to negotiate in the pursuit of greater social justice… After mass mobilization and strikes, the Polish Solidarity movement negotiated its way into power and transitioned Poland away from authoritarianism. Saul Alinsky, one of the United States' pioneering community activists, included negotiation as a critical step in his blueprint for action" (USIP, 2017, 5).

Weber goes further to argue that Gandhian nonviolence incorporates modern notions of negotiation and conflict resolution, as both are grounded in a win-win conflict framework. Vinthagen (2016), for his part, argues that nonviolent action is inherently dialogic. He proposes that all observed human behavior is a form of communication and that all nonviolent actions are a form of social conflict. Even if tactical actors protest without "listening," their goal is not to shout at trees and rocks but to reach the ears of another party. Therefore, all nonviolent methods unilaterally initiate a form of dialogue.

Smithey and Kurtz (2002, 319-359) offer a fascinating example of a wordless dialogue between Northern Ireland's Loyalists and Nationalists by way of nonviolent action. In the 1990s, the Loyalists of Ballyreagh theatrically abstained from a blockade of a nationalist parade. In response, at the parade, the nationalists self-policed their supporters to prevent conflict with the police. Over a period of months of reciprocal restraint, these parades were used as communication vehicles to build non-verbal trust that helped lead to spoken dialogue and negotiations.

However, because of the lack of universal agreement, we do not include dialogue and negotiation in our set of nonviolent methods.

---

47   Wanis-St. John and Rosen define leverage as the "manifestation of power in a negotiation. Leverage involves the ability to influence a negotiation outcome based on a party's ability to either confer or withhold benefits desired by the counterpart or impose or not impose costs on the counterpart."

Lobbying

Lobbying is a routinized activity in representative governance with known outcomes. Typically, lobbying entails citizens engaging an elected official at a public event or at their offices, or by means of a letter or phone call. Regardless of the content of the plea or demand, the outcome is fully in the hands of the representative who has the power to vote, and not the citizen lobbying. In practice, norms of personal conduct and communication can be disrupted and lobbying can be contentious, coercive, and still nonviolent. For example, in 2017, the author of this monograph participated in disruptive lobbying involving a teach-in conducted in a congressional office. The teach-in lasted for many hours until the lobbyists' demands for a public written statement were met. This teach-in was a form of creative and assertive lobbying that Medea Benjamin calls extreme lobbying.[48] Lobbying itself is generally not considered a method, but many nonviolent methods such as teach-ins, sit-ins, and call-ins are used to lobby elected officials.

Logistical Support Activities for Nonviolent Tactics

Tactical support activities are deployed to increase the chances of a nonviolent tactic succeeding. Because they are not weapons that target an adversary through the processes of persuasion, coercion, or manipulation, they are not defined as a nonviolent method in this monograph. However, some researchers (e.g., Beyerle, 2014) see them as important enough for the conduct of nonviolent conflict that they integrate them into the repertoire of nonviolent tactics. We have identified three types of support activities with specific examples:

PLANNING
- back-up plans
- evaluation
- messaging
- objectives
- scouting and assessment
- sequence planning for an action from beginning to end
- target analysis and selection
- timing, duration, and location

---

48 Labeled as such in conversations with Benjamin in 2018.

ORGANIZING AND LOGISTICS
- finance
- food and clothing
- fundraising
- internal and external media
- internal communications
- recruiting actionists, allies, and people for support roles
- resource design and preparation
- sound systems
- transport

TRAINING
- coordination of roles and leadership
- discipline and action guidelines, safety and security awareness, and preparation
- training coordination; venues, times, recruitment of trainers and trainees
- training guides, manuals, and videos
- training of trainers

Psychological Attack

Confrontational tactics that seek to weaken an opponent's will are commonplace in civil resistance. Sharp's classic list of methods includes rude gestures, mockumentaries, vituperative speech and writing, nudity, hoaxes, and rumors. These tactics have the potential power to cause deep psychological trauma or temporary discomfort. Followers of Gandhian nonviolence generally believe these methods, along with secrecy and property destruction, to be harmful to others and counter-productive to campaign success. Wilson (2017) distinguished between nefarious and virtuous nonviolent campaigns by the presence or absence of a "human rights ethos." This ethos is based on four principles of non-discrimination ("equal treatment of others"); non-repression ("goals that advance political rights and political autonomy for all"); non-exploitation ("solidarity with the persecuted, offering mutual aid, and reaching out to diverse groups of society to build shared understanding and trust"); and nonviolent means ("actions that do not threaten or do physical harm to others").

Such human rights yardsticks could be used to determine what methods might fall into the category of nonviolent action and whether intentions or agents behind such methods had virtuous or nefarious (anti-human rights ethos) ends in mind. This could help determine if they were part of a genuine civil resistance movement or not.

Actions Seemingly Without a Strategic Goal

Vinthagen (2015) writes about the functions of social norm regulation (e.g., dressing up in formal clothes or not striking back) and dialogical communication in nonviolent campaigns (e.g., actively listening to an adversary), which are important for normalizing nonviolent action in societies characterized by violence and oppression. This prefigurative and cultural work seeks to enact marginalized norms as routine behaviors without explicit strategic goals, but this may depend on the context. We leave these questions open, though this monograph does not incorporate such actions into its categorization of nonviolent methods.

In conclusion, many actions in civil resistance campaigns are not currently categorized as nonviolent tactics because there is significant debate about their function, the relationship between their means and ends, the nature of conflict and violence, and the role of communication and dialogue. It is beyond the scope of this monograph to determine if such actions can or should be part of the civil resistance repertoire. However, rather than seeing these different views of tactics as a sign of weakness or vagueness in the study of nonviolent civil resistance, we should interpret the diversity of creative actions and surrounding debates as a sign of the vibrancy and breadth of the field.

CHAPTER 7. Key Takeaways

This monograph sought to answer three basic questions:

1. What civil resistance tactics did Gene Sharp not identify, and what new methods of civil resistance have emerged or been identified since 1973? In response, this monograph introduces readers to a new and regularly updated database of more than 300 methods of nonviolent resistance (see Universe of Nonviolent Tactics Appendix).

2. What new categorization of tactics would be helpful in documenting this enormous area of human activity? In response, this monograph builds on Sharp's categorization, reviews other available classifications, and offers its own refined framework (included in Tables 1 and 4).

3. How can this new knowledge—tactics and classification—be helpful to practitioners and scholars of civil resistance, as well as to those who would like to assist nonviolent movements? The answer to this third question is provided in greater detail in the paragraphs below.

Takeaways for Activists

First, this study clearly demonstrates that many more nonviolent methods exist than have previously been documented. In fact, the author of the study collected information on more than 100 new tactics beyond the 198 identified in 1973 by Sharp.

This monograph selected and described only a limited number of new tactics (23) and mapped each of them onto the new framework in Table 4. The selected tactics cover a diverse range of characteristics. This is a testament to the ingenuity and creativity of activists around the world in developing and deploying new nonviolent tactics.

Activists can use this monograph's framework to better understand the variety of functions that nonviolent tactics perform. They can also use this framework to map out the tactics that they have deployed as part of their past and ongoing campaigns. This can help them visualize the extent to which their actions are tactically diverse and whether they might be placing too much emphasis on one set of tactics while intentionally or unintentionally disregarding others. This understanding, in turn, can help activists consider how their efforts can be re-balanced to increase the diversity of methods deployed and thus enhance their strategic leverage.

Practitioners should not conclude that certain tactics have lesser or greater value based on their categorization. Cataloguing civil resistance methods is not meant as a prescription or seal of approval for the actions identified in this monograph. Application of any nonviolent tactic should be determined by two key variables: appropriateness and efficacy. In other words, is the action the "right" or appropriate thing to do in the given circumstances, and is the action an "effective" thing to do to achieve short- and long-term goals?

It is also worth reiterating that many of the identified tactics can be categorized in more than one way. They can also have various helpful impacts for a movement depending on the movement's strategies and the overall context of the struggle. In addition to tactical preparation and skilled delivery, it will be the strategy behind nonviolent tactics that determines their value. This monograph's analytical mapping of tactics dissects the nature of various categories, which aims to help activists undertake more strategic assessment and planning.

Takeaways for Civil Resistance Scholars and Students

Categorizing tactics can be done in myriad ways. Strategists and social scientists are constantly discovering new patterns, relationships, and insights by re-classifying tactics based on various criteria, including dispersion/concentration, actors' motives, action audience, target object (will, body, or environment), stages of conflict, grievance issue, etc.

This monograph provides a number of examples of new methods to deepen understanding of two kinds of civil resistance actions: coercive or confrontational (threats and sanctions) on the one hand, and persuasive or constructive (appeals and rewards) on the other hand. Both are important.

In particular, this monograph explores in detail positive inducements such as appeals, refraining, and creative intervention, which can help researchers further explore the constructive dimension of various types of nonviolent methods. This monograph also aims to emphasize disruptive elements of civil resistance actions. Coercive nonviolent actions are often visible and dramatic (e.g., demonstrations, protests, and occupations). Thus, they can seemingly convey greater power and leverage of a movement than positive or constructive actions which, even if subtler, hidden, or less spectacular (e.g., appeals, persuasion, or alternative institution-building), can nevertheless have a profound impact on the trajectory of the struggle. To balance this, the framework presented in this monograph elucidates, among others, a new category of positive acts of omission entitled refraining, which is no less powerful than its disruptive counterparts and has been practiced for decades but until now had not been analytically identified or studied.

Researchers could expand on the framework presented in this monograph to investigate nonviolent campaigns and movements. This could include examining the examples, sequencing, effectiveness, and comparison of both coercive and persuasive tactics and thus provide insights into the overall conduct of a nonviolent struggle.

Furthermore, in Chapter 6, this monograph identifies a host of actions and dynamics in civil resistance campaigns that need further study (including the use of suicide, psychological intervention, property destruction, social norm regulation, utopian enactment, dialogical communication, third-party intervention, and everyday resistance) to determine their proper analytical place in the categorization of civil resistance methods.

More research, data collection, and analysis are required to clarify the criteria for defining nonviolent methods and tactics and to deepen our understanding of their underlying mechanisms. How should we address subcategories of civil disobedience tactics against unjust laws, which make up a huge array of illegal actions that have little in common with one another, other than that a government has labeled them illegal? What about tactics that are so context- specific, such as wade-ins (physical entrance to a prohibited space) to integrate pools and beaches in South Africa, that they are unlikely to be replicated in many other settings and thus scarcely warrant analytical attention or a framework to capture them? Should the method of banner display be subdivided into numerous categories of tactics because of the diversity of techniques, venues, and materials used, and the different deployment skills and resources that each of them requires? What would a gender perspective of understanding nonviolent tactics reveal for those studying civil resistance? Several questions remain to be studied and clarified.

This monograph aims to inspire civil resistance researchers and experts to document nonviolent tactics and map them into a universal framework that can offer a certain analytical order and clear systematization of the type, nature, and impact of nonviolent tactics.

Takeaways for Groups Interested in Supporting Nonviolent Movements

External actors can use this new framework to assess a movement's tactical diversity and how a movement's actions are distributed across the spectra of tactical categories. This may offer them information about the strengths and weaknesses of a movement's organizational capacity, strategic planning, and how a movement views the conditions it faces. This, in turn, can offer external actors hints about what to address in discussions with movement participants, as well as which tools and techniques external actors can employ to help a movement become more strategic in terms of design and/or deployment of their nonviolent tactics.

Concretely, this monograph provides an updated table and framework for understanding and analyzing nonviolent tactics. Any categorization of human endeavors is, to a certain extent, a simplification of reality, but given the extraordinary breadth of civil resistance, the methods template provided here can become an invaluable teaching tool. External trainers or advisors for a group of activists representing a specific campaign could, for example, use

Tables 1 and 4 as handouts to distribute as a teaching tool to facilitate reflection, analysis, and strategy with regards to nonviolent tactics.

In conclusion, exploring civil resistance tactics is not just a simple documentation or classification exercise. Studying each individual nonviolent tactic opens up a world of civil resistance stories in various places and times. It offers insight into people's ingenuity, perseverance, and resilience, often in the face of repression, demonstrating the desire to be creative and strategic in leading resistance struggles.

We hope this monograph and the ongoing Nonviolent Tactics Database will allow all of us to continue identifying, collecting, and cataloguing new tactics of civil resistance that activists and organizers around the world use in their ongoing struggles for rights, freedom, justice, and sustainability.

Cited Bibliography

Ackerman, Peter and Jack DuVall. *A Force More Powerful: A Century of Nonviolent Conflict.* New York, NY: Palgrave, 2000.

Ackerman, Peter. "Skills or Conditions: What Key Factors Shape the Success or Failure of Civil Resistance?" Conference on Civil Resistance and Power Politics, Oxford University (March 15-18, 2007), pp. 1-9. Retrieved from: **https://www.nonviolent-conflict.org/resource/skills-conditions-key-factors-shape-success-failure-civil-resistance/**

Ackerman, Peter and Christopher Kruegler. *Strategic Nonviolent Conflict: The Dynamics of People Power in the Twentieth Century.* Westport, CT: Praeger Publishers, 1994.

Ackerman, Peter and Hardy Merriman. "The Checklist for Ending Tyranny" in Mathew Burrows and Maria J. Stephan (eds.), *Is Authoritarianism Staging a Comeback?* Washington, DC: The Atlantic Council, 2015.

"Airport Workers' Strikes Suspended at Newark Liberty, 3 Other Airports," *News12 New Jersey*, July 12, 2017. Retrieved from: **http://newjersey.news12.com/story/35862766/airport-workers-strikes-suspended-at-newark-liberty-3-other-airports**

Amnesty International UK. "Huge Response to Crowdfunded Newspaper Ads Campaign Opposing Repeal of Human Rights Act," May 20, 2015. Retrieved from: **https://www.amnesty.org.uk/press-releases/huge-response-crowdfunded-newspaper-ads-campaign-opposing-repeal-human-rights-act**

Awad, Mubarak and Laura Bain. *Organizing Tactics for Nonviolent Action: Fasting.* Washington, DC: Nonviolence International, 1995.

Balch, Oliver. "New Hope for Argentina in the Recovered Factory Movement," *The Guardian*, March 12, 2013. Retrieved from: **https://www.theguardian.com/sustainable-business/argentina-recovered-factory-movement**

Bartkowski, Maciej. "How Online Courses on Civil Resistance Can Make Real Impact," *ICNC Minds of the Movement*, February 13, 2019. Retrieved from: **https://www.nonviolent-conflict.org/blog_post/online-courses-civil-resistance-can-make-real-impact/**

Bartkowski, Maciej. *Recovering Nonviolent History: Civil Resistance in Liberation Struggles.* Boulder, CO: Lynne Rienner Publishers, 2013.

Beer (1995), Mainstreaming Peace Teams, Collated and Published by Nonviolence International.

Beyerle, Shaazka. *Curtailing Corruption: People Power for Accountability and Justice.* Boulder, CO: Lynne Rienner Publishers, 2014.

Bloch, Nadine. *Education and Training in Nonviolent Resistance.* Washington, DC: United States Institute for Peace, 2016.

Bloch, Nadine. "The Arts of Protest: Creative Cultural Resistance." ICNC Webinar. Retrieved from: **https://www.nonviolent-conflict.org/the-arts-of-protest-creative-cultural-resistance/**

Bond, Doug. "Nonviolent Direct Action and the Diffusion of Power" in Paul Wehr et. al. (eds.), *Justice Without Violence.* Boulder, CO: Lynne Rienner Publishers, 1994, pp. 59-79.

Bond, Doug, et. al., "Mapping Mass Political Conflict and Civil Society: Issues and prospects for the automated development of event data." *Journal of Conflict Resolution*, vol. 41, Aug 1997.

Boserup, Anders and Andrew Mack. *War without Weapons: Non-violence in National Defense.* New York, NY: Schocken, 1975.

Browder, Bill. "The Russians Killed My Lawyer. This Is How I Got Congress to Avenge Him," *Politico*, February 3, 2015. Retrieved from: **https://www.politico.com/magazine/story/2015/02/sergei-magnitsky-murder-114878**

Burrowes, Robert J. "Cross-border Nonviolent Intervention: A Typology" in Yeshua Moser-Puangsuwan and Thomas Weber (eds.), *Nonviolent Intervention Across Borders: A Recurrent Vision.* Honolulu, HI: University of Hawai'i Press, 2000.

Burrowes, Robert J. *The Strategy of Nonviolent Defense: A Gandhian Approach.* Albany, NY: State University of New York Press, 1995.

Canning, Doyle and Patrick Reinsborough. "Changing the Story: Story-Based Strategies for Direct Action Design," Smart Meme, May 2008. Retrieved from: **https://inthemiddleofthewhirlwind.wordpress.com/changing-the-story/**

Center for Artistic Activism and the Yes Lab. Actipedia. Retrieved from: **https://actipedia.org/**

Chenoweth, Erica. "Trends in Civil Resistance and Authoritarian Responses" in Mathew Burrows and Maria J. Stephan (eds.), *Is Authoritarianism Staging a Comeback?* Washington, DC: The Atlantic Council, 2015, pp. 53-62.

Chenoweth, Erica and Maria Stephan. *Why Civil Resistance Works: The Strategic Logic of Nonviolent Conflict.* New York, NY: Columbia University Press, 2011.

Chenoweth, Erica and Maria Stephan. "How the world is proving Martin Luther King right about nonviolence," *Washington Post*, January 18, 2016.

Christoff, Stefan. "Cacerolazo." Beautiful Trouble. Retrieved from: **http://beautifultrouble.org/tactic/cacerolazo/**

Clark, Howard (ed.). *People Power: Unarmed Resistance and Global Solidarity.* London, UK: Pluto Press, 2009.

Cortright, David. *Peace: A History of Movements and Ideas.* Cambridge, UK: Cambridge University Press, 2008.

Crawford-Brown, Terry. "International Sanctions Against Israeli Banks," Just World Education, August 4, 2017. Retrieved from: **http://justworldeducational.org/2017/08/international-sanctions-israeli-banks/**

Curle, Adam. *Making Peace.* London, UK: Tavistock Publications, 1971.

Deming, Barbara. *On Revolution and Equilibrium.* New York, NY: A. J. Muste Memorial Institute, 1971.

Dorjee, Tenzin. *The Tibetan Nonviolent Struggle: A Strategic and Historical Analysis.* Washington, DC: ICNC Press, 2015.

Dudouet, Véronique (ed.). *Civil Resistance and Conflict Transformation: Transitions from Armed to Nonviolent Struggle.* Abingdon, UK: Routledge, 2014.

Dudouet, Véronique. *Powering to Peace: Integrated Civil Resistance and Peacebuilding Strategies.* Washington, DC: ICNC Press, 2017. Retrieved from: **https://www.nonviolent-conflict.org/powering-peace-integrated-civil-resistance-peacebuilding-strategies**

Dudouet, Véronique. "Sources, Functions and Dilemmas of External Assistance to Civil Resistance Movements," in Kurt Schock (ed.) Civil Resistance: Comparative Perspectives on Nonviolent Struggle. Minneapolis, MN: University of Minnesota Press, 2015.

Ebert, Theodore. *Gewaltfreier Aufstand: Alternative zum Bürgerkrieg. (Nonviolent Uprising: Alternatives to Civil War).* Hamburg, Germany: Fischer Verlag, 1970.

EFE. "Activists in Hong Kong Call for End to Shark Fin Trade ahead of New Year," January 30, 2016. Retrieved from: **https://www.efe.com/efe/english/life/activists-in-hong-kong-call-for-end-to-shark-fin-trade-ahead-of-new-year/50000263-2825615**

French, Amber. "How Do Nonviolent Movements Shape History? An Interview with Jacques Semelin," Minds of the Movement, October 16, 2017. Retrieved from: **https://www.nonviolent-conflict.org/blog_post/nonviolent-movements-shape-history-interview-jacques-semelin/**

"MEPs Cut EU Parliament Interpreting Service to Back Strikers," France24, July 3, 2018. Retrieved from: **http://www.france24.com/en/20180703-meps-cut-eu-parliament-interpreting-service-back-strikers**

Garano, Lorna. "Speaking Mirth to Power," Popular Resistance, June 26, 2016. Retrieved from: **https://popularresistance.org/speaking-mirth-to-power/**

Garofoli, Joe. "Critical Mass Turns 10," *San Francisco Chronicle*, September 28, 2002. Retrieved from: **https://www.sfgate.com/politics/joegarofoli/article/Critical-Mass-turns-10-A-decade-of-defiance-2767020.php**

Geddie, John. "Hong Kong students take protest to virtual world," Reuters, October 31, 2019. Retrieved from: **https://web.archive.org/web/20191031181503/https://www.asiaone.com/digital/hong-kong-students-take-protest-virtual-world**.

Goldman, David and Jose Pagliery. "#JeSuisCharlie Becomes One of Most Popular Hashtags in Twitter's History," *CNN*, January 9, 2015. Retrieved from: **https://money.cnn.com/2015/01/09/technology/social/jesuis-charlie-hashtag-twitter/index.html**

Green, Matthew. "Ghana Puts Faith in Humble Text Message," *Financial Times*, December 8, 2008. Retrieved from: **https://www.ft.com/content/04a981ce-c553-11dd-b516-000077b07658**

Hallward, Maia Carter, and Julie M. Norman (eds.). *Understanding Nonviolence: Contours and Contexts*. Cambridge, UK: Polity, 2015.

Harrebye, Silas F. *Social Change and Creative Activism in the 21st Century*. New York, NY: Palgrave Macmillan, 2016.

Hastings, Tom. "Property Damage, Violence, Nonviolent Action, and Strategy." *Minds of the Movement* (blog). ICNC, June 2, 2020. **https://www.nonviolent-conflict.org/blog_post/property-damage-violence-nonviolent-action-and-strategy/**

Harvard Digital Collection. "Chilean Protest Murals." Retrieved from: **http://www.jr-art.net**

Hunter, Daniel and George Lakey. *Opening Space for Democracy: Training Manual for Third-Party Nonviolent Intervention*. Philadelphia, PA: Training for Change, 2003.

Jordan, John. "Clandestine Insurgent Rebel Clown Army." Beautiful Trouble. Retrieved from: **https://www.beautifultrouble.org/toolbox/#/tool/clandestine-insurgent-rebel-clown-army**

Joyce, Mary. "Civil Resistance 2.0: Digital Enhancements to the 198 Nonviolent Methods." ICNC Webinar. Retrieved from: **https://www.nonviolent-conflict.org/civil-resistance-2-0-digital-enhancements-to-the-198-nonviolent-methods/**

Khatib, Kate, et. al. *We Are Many: Reflections on Movement Strategy from Occupation to Liberation*. Chico, CA: AK Press, 2012.

King, Mary Elizabeth. *Gandhian Nonviolent Struggle and Untouchability in South India: The 1924-1925 Vykom Satyagraha and the Mechanisms of Change*. Oxford: Oxford University Press, 2015.

Kurtz, Mariam M. and Lester R. Kurtz. *Women, War, and Violence: Topography, Resistance, and Hope, volume II*. Westport, CT: Praeger, 2015.

La Porte, Amy. "Muslim Leaders Refuse to Bury French Priest Killer," *CNN*, August 1, 2016. Retrieved from: **https://www.cnn.com/2016/07/30/europe/priest-killer-burial-refused/index.html**

Lakey, George. "The Sociological Mechanisms of Nonviolent Action." Peace Research Review 2 (1968), pp. 1-102.

Lee, Hyun. "South Korea's Historic 'One Million People Protest' to Oust Washington's Puppet President Park Geun-hye," *Global Research*, November 14, 2016. Retrieved from: **https://www.globalresearch.ca/south-koreas-historic-one-million-people-protest-to-oust-washingtons-puppet-president-park-geun-hye/5556808**

Madden, Richard. "London: How cyclists around the world put a spoke in the motorist's wheel," *The Daily Telegraph*. December 15, 2003. Retrieved from: **https://www.telegraph.co.uk/travel/729324/London-How-cyclists-around-the-world-put-a-spoke-in-the-motorists-wheel.html**

Mahony, Liam and Luis Enrique Eguren. *Unarmed Bodyguards: International Accompaniment for the Protection of Human Rights*. Boulder, CO: Lynne Rienner Publishers, 1997.

Maney, Gregory M., et. al. (eds.). *Strategies for Social Change*. Minneapolis, MN: University of Minnesota Press, 2012.

Matthews, David. "Mexican Protestors are Striking Back at Donald Trump—with Video Games," September 2, 2015. Retrieved from: **https://splinternews.com/mexican-programmers-are-striking-back-at-donald-trump-w-1793850467**

McCarthy, Ronald et. al. (eds.). *Protest, Power, and Change: An Encyclopedia of Nonviolent Action from Act-Up to Women's Suffrage*. New York, NY: Garland Publishing, 1997.

Mitchell, Dave O. and Andrew Boyd. "Tactic: Flash Mob." Retrieved from: **https://www.beautifultrouble.org/toolbox/#/tool/flash-mob**

Moser, Yeshua. *Organizing Tactics for Nonviolent Action: Organizing Walks and Pilgrimages*. Washington, DC: Nonviolence International, 1993.

Noplatform forIMF [YouTube user]. "Mic-Check Disruption of the Speech of IMF Managing Director, Christine Lagarde, 2013." Retrieved from: **https://www.youtube.com/watch?v=axLA-qG3EWg**

Nurhan, Abujidi. *Urbicide in Palestine: Spaces of Oppression and Resilience*. New York: Routledge, 2014.

Powers, Roger et. al. (eds.). *Protest, Power, and Change: An Encyclopedia of Nonviolent Action from Act-Up to Women's Suffrage*. New York, NY: Garland Publishing, 1997.

Principe, Marie. *Women in Nonviolent Movements*. Washington, DC: United States Institute for Peace, 2016. Retrieved from: **https://www.usip.org/publications/2016/12/women-nonviolent-movements**

Rigby, Andrew. *Palestinian Resistance and Nonviolence*. East Jerusalem: PASSIA, 2010. Retrieved from: **https://www.academia.edu/16293156/Palestinian_Resistance_and_Nonviolence**

Rigby, Andrew and Marwan Darweish. *Popular Protest in Palestine: The History and Uncertain Future of Unarmed Resistance*. London, UK: Pluto Press, 2015.

Schell, Jonathan. *The Unconquerable World: Power, Nonviolence, and the Will of the People*. New York: Metropolitan Books, 2003.

Schelling, Thomas C. "Some Questions on Civilian Defence," in Adam Roberts, ed., *Civilian Resistance as a National Defence: Non-violent Action against Aggression*. Harrisburg, PA: Stackpole Books, 1968.

Schlegel, Ivy. "Palm Oil Scorecard: Are Brands Doing Enough for Indonesia's Rainforests?" Greenpeace.com. March 9, 2016. Retrieved from: **https://www.greenpeace.org/usa/palm-oil-scorecard-are-brands-doing-enough-for-indonesias-rainforests/**

Schock, Kurt. *Civil Resistance Today.* Cambridge, UK: Polity, 2015.

Schock, Kurt (ed.). *Civil Resistance: Comparative Perspectives on Nonviolent Struggle.* Minneapolis, MN: University of Minnesota Press, 2015.

Schock, Kurt. "Land Struggles in the Global South: Strategic Innovations in Brazil and India," in Maney, Gregory M., et. al. (eds.), *Strategies for Social Change.* Minneapolis, MN: University of Minnesota Press, 2012.

Schock, Kurt. *Unarmed Insurrections: People Power Movements in Nondemocracies.* Minneapolis, MN: University of Minnesota Press, 2005.

Scott, James. "Everyday Forms of Resistance." *Copenhagen Papers in East and Southeast Asian Studies*, vol. 4, May 1989, pp. 55-56.

Shaou, Patrick and Whea Dodge. "Imagining Dissent: Contesting the Façade of Harmony through Art in China," in Stephen John Hartnett et. al. (eds.) *Imagining China: Rhetorics of Nationalism in an Age of Globalization.* East Lansing, MI: Michigan State University Press, 2017.

Sharp, Gene. *Gandhi as a Political Strategist.* Boston, MA: Porter Sargent Publishers, 1979.

Sharp, Gene. *The Politics of Nonviolent Action, Part Two: The Methods of Nonviolent Action.* Boston, MA: Porter Sargent Publishers, 1973.

Sharp, Gene. *Waging Nonviolent Struggle, 20th Century Practice and 21st Century Potential.* Manchester, NH: Extending Horizons Books, 2005.

Smithey, Lee A. and Lester R. Kurtz. "Parading Persuasion: Nonviolent Collective Action as Discourse in Northern Ireland," in Patrick G. Coy (ed.), *Consensus Decision Making, Northern Ireland and Indigenous Movements.* West Yorkshire, UK: Emerald Group Publishing Ltd., 2002.

Taylor, Adam. "Intruders Thought Stealing a Giant Gold Mace Would Disrupt Nigeria's Parliament. It Didn't Work," *The Washington Post.* April 19, 2018. Retrieved from: **https://www.washingtonpost.com/news/worldviews/wp/2018/04/19/intruders-thought-stealing-a-giant-gold-mace-would-disrupt-nigerias-parliament-it-didnt-work/?noredirect=on&utm_term=.afc2152e9b03**

Ulmer, Alexandra. "Venezuelans Revel in Pots-and-Pans Protests after Maduro Humiliation," Reuters. September 9, 2016. Retrieved from: **http://www.reuters.com/article/us-venezuela-politics-pots-idUSKCN11F22M**

Vinthagen, Stellan. *A Theory of Nonviolent Action: How Civil Resistance Works.* London, UK: Zed Books, 2015.

Wanis-St. John, Anthony and Noah Rose. *Negotiating Civil Resistance.* Washington, DC: United States Institute for Peace, 2017. Retrieved from: **https://www.usip.org/sites/default/files/2017-07/pw129-negotiating-civil-resistance.pdf**

Wilson, Elizabeth W. *People Power and International Human Rights Law: Creating a Legal Framework.* Washington, DC: ICNC Press, 2017. Retrieved from: **https://www.nonviolent-conflict.org/resource/people-power-movements-international-human-rights-creating-legal-framework/**

Zunes, Stephen. *Civil Resistance Against Coups: A Comparative and Historical Perspective.* Washington, DC: ICNC Press, 2017. Retrieved from: **https://www.nonviolent-conflict.org/resource/civil-resistance-coups-comparative-historical-perspective/**

APPENDIX

Universe of Nonviolent Tactics

The following Appendix presents 346 tactics of nonviolent resistance, which comprises Sharp's 198 methods from 1973, as well as the new nonviolent tactics included in the Nonviolent Tactics Database.[49] The Appendix also presents the refined categorization of all old and new nonviolent methods. There are many categorization systems to organize methods of nonviolent resistance as outlined in this monograph (see Chapter 3 and 4). The tactics are organized in this Appendix through the categorization hierarchy presented in this monograph as illustrated in the chart below.

The tactic number on the far right of each method refers to the unique identification number assigned to the tactic in the Nonviolent Tactics Database.

The red numbers in parentheticals are the original tactic numbers that Sharp assigned for each of his 198 methods in 1973.

Expression/Protest and Appeal
(HOW ONE SAYS SOMETHING)

Expressive Tactics Using Medium of the Human Person

MOVEMENTS & GESTURES

Dance: Performing or participating in a form of dance to demonstrate discontent/resilience/agreement — 1

Rude gestures (30): Using hand or arm gestures that are considered rude or anti-social in the social context — 2

Martial arts: Practicing martial arts as a means of protest or appeal — 3

Human banner: Using human bodies to make a picture or spell a word, usually visible from above — 65

Hand gesture: Hand gestures (by an individual or a group) that are used to convey opposition — 307

Human chain: Many people join hands to form a giant line as a demonstration of political solidarity — 308

Kneeling: Kneeling in places or during a time when it is not socially appropriate to do so — 309

Body percussion: Creating man-made sounds meant to display approval, disapproval, or unification (e.g., applause) — 310

---

49 For more information, see: **https://www.tactics.nonviolenceinternational.net/**.

PROCESSIONS

Marches (38): A group of people walking together to reach a particular point as a means of protest or appeal 4

Parades (39): Similar to a march, but the point of destination is not politically significant; it is only a convenient place of termination 5

Religious processions (40): A march or a parade with a religious character 6

Pilgrimages (41): A walk (by an individual or a group) that has a significant moral and/or religious aspect 7

Picketing (16): Congregating outside a place to protest and deter entry—hence, crossing the picket line 10

Walk and trek: A long walk or journey meant to increase public awareness and/or demonstrate support for or opposition against a specific cause/group/law/etc.; the route is important, as a more publicly visible passage is more likely to raise awareness 11

PUBLIC ASSEMBLIES

Deputations (13): A representative delegation meeting with an opposing party in order to present grievances or to propose new policy 9

"Live crowd 'choreography' through crowd-sourced data": Using apps to coordinate the movement of the crowd 12

Check-ins: Using social networking sites to 'check in' at a protest and show your support 13

Assemblies of protest or support (47): A gathering of protest/dissent that occurs at places important to the cause of the demonstration (e.g., courthouse steps) 14

Protest meetings (48): Similar to an assembly of protest or support, but occurring wherever is convenient 15

Camouflaged meetings of protest (49): Protest meetings that are presented as something else (e.g., sporting event, religious ceremony, etc.), often in order to avoid legal repercussions 16

Group lobbying (15): A collective group of constituents presents their argument for a specific issue to their designated parliamentary representative 17

Vigil (34): A period of prayer or keeping watch to honor some person or event 18

Coordinated worldwide demonstrations: Mass international demonstrations that occur simultaneously in order to draw extensive attention to a particular issue 19

RITUALS & TRADITIONS

Growing/shaving hair as protest: Common expression of mourning or criticism of an action, policy, etc. 20

Wearing traditional or historical clothing or costumes: Appeals to tradition or history 21

National anthem protests: Expressing some kind of dissent during the performance of a national anthem 22

Invocation of magic: The practice of magic used to condemn the actions of an individual or group 23

Prayer and worship (20): Demonstrating moral disapproval or political protest through religious acts 24

HONORING THE DEAD

Political mourning (43): Utilizing symbols of mourning such as grief and loss to demonstrate dissent with a certain policy, event, or action 25

Mock funerals (44): Organizing a fake funeral that grieves opponents' violation of some virtue or belief 26

Demonstrative funerals (45): Transformation of an actual funeral into a protest, which is especially effective when honoring a victim who died at the hands of opponents 27

Homage at burial places (46): Demonstration at the burial site of a person who was symbolic and/or influential to the cause behind the protest 28

PERFORMANCE

Mock awards (14): Creation of fictional awards for the sake of making a statement on an issue 29

Mock tribunals: Unofficial public tribunals for victims or protesters to share feelings and thoughts about certain polices/actions 31

Flash mobs/smart mobs: Group gathers in a public place and performs a seemingly out of place action (i.e., choreographed dance) for a brief period, then disperses 32

Humorous skits and pranks (35): Protest through the use of comedy or satire 33

Traditional theater (36): Using theater sketches, plays, and skits to increase awareness, spread information, and/or protest or appeal 34

Destruction of own property (23): Willingly destroying one's own property as an act of protest/appeal 35

One-person protest (with or without aggregation): A single activist doing some action of protest/appeal that can often provide observers with the opportunity to join 36

Wearing/displaying a single color: Wearing a single color on a pre-determined day to express support for a movement and/or discontent with an individual or government 311

WITHDRAWAL & RENUNCIATION

Walk-outs (51): An act of protest/appeal in which participants walk out during a meeting, assembly, etc.   40

Silence (52): Maintaining silence in response to a speaker or event; often used to convey moral condemnation   41

Renouncing honors (53): Giving up an honor/award as an act of protest or appeal   42

Turning one's back (54): Turning away when an opponent speaks or performs; can be singular or en masse   43

PRESSURE ON INDIVIDUALS

"Haunting" officials (31): Activists follow officials and remind them of their presence and dedication to the cause   44

Taunting officials (32): Straightforward mockery of an official in a public space   45

Fraternization (33): Socializing with police or soldiers in an attempt to mitigate their actions and/or persuade them to join the cause   46

Expressive Tactics using Medium of Things

SOUND & MUSIC

Symbolic sounds (28): Use of sounds without language to set a tone or send a message   49

Cacerolazo: Banging on pots and pans as part of a march or similar event   50

Car horns: Repeated use of car horns in an organized fashion to raise awareness/voice discontent   51

Whistles: The use of whistles or the technique of whistling to create noise   52

Drumming: Creating noise/rhythms that amplify chanting/singing/shouting   53

Musical instruments (36): Delivering protest or appeal through instruments producing sound that is presented to the public   93

2-DIMENSIONAL ARTS & MATERIALS

Banners, posters, and other displayed communications (8): Portable written, painted, or printed communication that is typically displayed in public and used to send or amplify a message   54

Paint as protest (26): Graffiti, painting over signs, etc.   55

Displays of flags and symbolic colors (18): Expression of political dissent by displaying/wearing a country's flag or symbolic colors, a group's symbolic flags or colors, etc.   56

Wearing of symbols (19): Expression of political dissent by wearing symbolic clothing, colors, items, etc.   57

Symbolic lights (24): Using lights as expression (for example, turning off lights, torches, candles, etc. en masse)   58

Displays of portraits (25): Displaying portraits in a public space, often paired with a vigil or similar event   59

Comics: Comics that criticize/mock/draw attention to individuals, groups, companies, or particular issues   61

Stickers: Displaying stickers that show support/opposition   62

Logos: Creating or repurposing logos to convey a message/prove a point   63

Buttons: Displaying buttons that show support/opposition   224

Makeup/face painting: Using makeup or face paint to demonstrate or display a message, or to make a point   312

3-DIMENSIONAL ARTS & MATERIALS

Motorcades (42): Similar to a march or parade but involves participants driving cars at a slow speed rather than walking   8

Food waste (or other farm goods) as protest: Using food waste as a form of protest/appeal   38

Mailing symbolic items (21): Shipping an item that has a particular symbolic meaning as an act of protest   47

Delivering symbolic objects (21): Dropping off significant objects to an opponent   66

Puppets: Using puppets (and puppet shows) to exemplify a message, make fun of opponents, or critique a particular group/individual/issue   67

Props: The use of props to add creativity and/or to emphasize the reason or cause behind a protest   68

Costumes: Dressing up in a costume relevant to the issue in order to draw attention   69

Mascots: Dressing up as a mascot to draw attention to an issue   70

Sculpture: Producing sculptures to emphasize an issue, to memorialize and/or honor a person relevant to the cause, to demonstrate a point, and/or to call out an opponent   71

Vehicles, with 2D and 3D art: Turning vehicles (trucks, cars, boats, hot air balloons, planes, etc.) into mobile message-delivering/information-spreading mechanisms   72

Expressive Tactics Using Medium of Electronic Communication

RECORDING & DISTRIBUTING NEWS OF NVA

Livestreaming: The live public broadcasting of an event, incident, or protest   73

Short form digital video: A brief video detailing the issue that people are protesting for/against   74

Social media photo campaign: Promoting a particular image through social media platforms (for example, changing profile pictures)   75

Database leaks: Releasing entire digital archives of secret/classified materials in order to educate the public and/or increase awareness   313

CROWDSOURCING INFORMATION

Sousveillance: Covert surveillance by citizens, frequently of authorities — 76

Maps and maptivism: Using maps, typically digital ones, to crowdsource data or information — 77

Digital file sharing applications: Peer-to-peer file-sharing (uTorrent, etc.) — 78

CREATING ONLINE DIGITAL CONTENT

Blogging/writing/commenting/tweeting: Creating online written content that addresses particular issues, which is especially useful if it is too dangerous to speak out or protest in person — 80

Digital video and audio art: Using media forms such as videos, photos, photos of art, digital art, animations, and silent videos to protest/appeal — 81

Digital games: Digital games that are used to criticize opponents and their ideas or to model a new behavior or institution — 314

FALSE, IMAGINARY INFORMATION

Creating faux identities, websites, videos: Creating some kind of hoax or fake information that is intended to mock opponents and/or shock the public — 82

Mockumentaries: A documentary that uses humor and parody to mock an opponent or issue — 83

Mock documents (government forms): Constructing mock documents or forms for use by the public — 84

Deliberately fake money: Creating false currency that can be used to combat corruption, spread awareness about the issue, etc. — 85

MASS ACTION

SMS/email/social media bombing: Using text messaging, email, or social media functions to send messages en masse to a target — 86

Forwarding information, retweeting, re-posting, sharing: Sharing information and raising awareness through social media or other messaging systems — 87

Trend a hashtag: Using a social media platform's hashtag feature to call attention to an issue or event (#) — 88

Influencing Internet search engines: Changing the results of a search engine for a specific term/person — 89

"Nonviolently 'hijacking' social media": Hacking, posting on, exposing, and/or disabling the social media accounts of an opponent — 90

Social media "challenges": Using social media to call others to action on a mass scale — 91

Solidarity telethon: Mass calls to spread information and solidarity — 315

Product review hijacking: Negatively or positively mass-reviewing a product — 316

Expressive Tactics using Medium of Human Language

Singing (37): Using song as a way to express a particular viewpoint or to drown out opponents' speech — 48

Changing narratives/flipping scripts/editing song lyrics, etc.: Altering an existing narrative, song, script, etc. to exemplify how the original was incorrect, offensive, misleading, etc. — 64

Teach-ins (50): Educating attendees on a topic by allowing speakers representing various viewpoints to talk without strict limits on time or scope and encouraging audience engagement; popularized during the Vietnam War — 92

Skywriting and earthwriting (12): Writing messages in the sky or on the earth so they are visible from afar — 94

Slogans, caricatures, and symbols (7): Simple messages or symbols that are written, painted, printed, mimed, gestured, drawn, spoken, etc. — 95

Letters of opposition or support (2): Letters signed by individuals and/or organizations taking a stance on an issue — 96

Declarations by organizations and institutions (3): Statements that not only express a viewpoint, but place blame on a wrongdoer and/or declare an intent to take action — 97

Signed public statements (4): Statement for the general public signed by individuals and/or organizations — 98

Declarations of indictment and intention (5): Statements that declare an intention rather than merely statements of expression — 99

Group or mass petitions (6): Written requests with a specific purpose that have a large number of signatories — 100

Public written advertisements: Advertisements that provide a service, send a message, or highlight a particular issue — 101

Distributing dissenting leaflets and pamphlets (9): Distributing written material to express dissent or opposition — 102

Newspapers and journals (10): Expressing dissent or opposition through articles in newspapers, journals, and other publications — 103

Public speeches (1): Prepared or spontaneous addresses delivered as an act of opposition, protest, support, etc. — 104

Call and response: Chants or slogans punctuated by responses from the listeners — 105

Chanting: Group shouting with rhythmic, repetitive words and sounds, with or without a melody — 106

Call-in/phone march: Organizing mass phone calls to an official or authority — 108

Poetry/spoken word: Writing and performing poetry as a way to fight back against violence and the silencing of voices — 109

People's mic: Using a large group of people to amplify a message by shouting out the same message in waves (similar to call and response) — 110

Coded language: Creating a linguistic code to circumvent censorship — 111

Rude/transgressive language: Swearing or using offensive language to demonstrate a point or prevent opponents from talking — 112

Counter cat-calling: Responding to cat-calling in a loud and expressive fashion to draw attention to public sexual harassment — 317

Self disclosure: Speaking out against egregious crimes by revealing personal grievances — 319

Publishing dissenting literature (9): Writing educational or training material that relates to the strategies of resistance — 346

Acts of Omission
Noncooperation: Coercive Acts
(HOW ONE DOESN'T DO SOMETHING)

Social Noncooperation

OSTRACISM OF PERSONS

Social boycott (55): Refusal to engage with a particular person or group of persons — 113

Selective social boycott (56): Refusal to partake in a specific type of social behavior with a particular person or group of persons — 114

Lysistratic nonaction (57): Refusal of sex until demands are met — 115

Excommunication (58): Excluding someone from religious services, ceremonies, and practices — 116

Interdict (59): Suspension of religious services in a certain region until some form of political or social change comes into effect — 117

NONCOOPERATION WITH SOCIAL EVENTS, CUSTOMS & INSTITUTIONS

Suspension of social and sports activities (60): Refusal to arrange or participate in social activities — 118

Boycott of social affairs (61): Refusal to attend certain types of social events — 119

Student strike (62): Refusal to attend class — 120

Withdrawal from social institutions (64): Resigning from or refusing to participate in certain institutions — 121

Refusal of pledges or oaths: Withholding promises or avowals — 123

WITHDRAWAL FROM THE SOCIAL SYSTEM

Stay-at-home (65): Organized act of staying at home; usually, but not always, during working hours — 124

Total personal noncooperation (66): A prisoner's complete refusal to take any action, including eating, drinking, or even moving one's body — 125

"Flight" of workers (67): Workers stop working and leave home, but do not yet impose demands — 126

Sanctuary (68): Fleeing to a place where one cannot be removed due to religious, legal, moral, or social restrictions — 127

Collective disappearance (69): Temporary abandonment of a place by a population — 128

Protest emigration (hijrat) (70): Voluntary exile from a place — 129

Ghost town: Large portions of the population stay home instead of going to work or school — 320

Economic Noncooperation: Boycotts

ACTION BY CONSUMERS

Consumers' boycott (71): Consumer refusal to purchase certain goods or a certain class of goods — 130

Nonconsumption of boycotted goods (72): Refusal to use or consume boycotted goods that one has already purchased — 131

Policy of austerity (73): Giving up personal luxuries either for symbolic reasons or as a boycott — 132

Rent withholding (74): Refusal to pay rent to a landlord or property owner — 133

Refusal to rent (75): Refusal to rent a building or land in order to protest against the owner or landlord — 134

National consumers' boycott (76): Boycott that extends to an entire nation and the products produced there — 135

International consumers' boycott (77): Boycott of a nation's goods/services that is enforced by multiple nations — 136

Coin hoarding: An effort to not spend a particular form of currency in hopes that it will take large amounts of cash out of circulation — 321

ACTION BY WORKERS & PRODUCERS

Producers' boycott (79): Producers refuse to create, sell, or deliver their products — 137

Workmen's boycott (78): Workers refuse to use supplies or tools that were produced under certain circumstances — 322

ACTION BY MIDDLEMEN

Suppliers' and handlers' boycott (80): 'Middlemen' refuse to accommodate the shipping and processing of a product — 138

ACTION BY OWNERS & MANAGEMENT

Traders' boycott (81): Retail outlets refuse to buy, sell, or deliver a particular product — 139

Refusal to let or sell property (82): Refusal of a property owner to rent or sell property to specific persons or groups — 140

Lockout (83): Employer temporarily closes the workplace in order to put pressure on employees — 141

Refusal of industrial assistance (84): Organization refuses to produce economic/technical services to opponent — 142

Merchants' "general strike" (85): Merchants or retailers close down their businesses to slow or stop the economic flow — 143

ACTION BY HOLDERS OF FINANCIAL RESOURCES

Withdrawal of bank deposits (86): Terminating financial cooperation 144

Refusal to pay fees, dues, and assessments (87): Refusing to pay a monetary sum to a certain establishment, government, etc. as an act of protest or appeal 145

Refusal to pay debts or interest (88): Not submitting what is owed 146

Severance of funds and credit (89): Cutting off sources of money for opponents 147

Revenue refusal (90): Usually a refusal to pay proceeds to the government (i.e., taxes or licenses) 148

Divestment: Institutional separation from corporations whose actions investors find objectionable 323

ACTION BY GOVERNMENTS

Domestic embargo (92): Government that boycotts a particular institution or opponent within its borders 149

Blacklisting of traders (93): Prohibiting trade with particular firms or individuals 150

International sellers' embargo (94): Government disallows selling a product to a country 151

International buyers' embargo (95): Government disallows buying a product from a country 152

International trade embargo (96): Combination of international sellers' embargo and international buyers' embargo 153

Economic Noncooperation: Strikes

SYMBOLIC STRIKES

Protest strike (97): Strike performed for a set period of time with the purpose of making a statement rather than achieving a specific goal 154

Quickie walkout (lightning strike) (98): Short, unplanned strikes often undertaken when more formal strikes are illegal or impractical 155

AGRICULTURAL STRIKES

Peasant strike (99): Refusal of peasants to cooperate with landlords 156

Farm workers' strike (100): Strike by hired agricultural workers 157

STRIKES BY SPECIAL GROUPS

Refusal of impressed labor (101): Refusal of slaves and coerced laborers to work — 158

Prisoners' strike (102): Refusal by prisoners to participate in labor — 159

Craft strike (103): Strike by workers of the same craft; usually associated with a craft union — 160

Professional strike (104): Strike undertaken by members of a specific profession — 161

Statewide strikes: A statewide strike that incorporates refusing to go to school, attend work, open shops, etc. — 324

ORDINARY INDUSTRIAL STRIKES

Establishment strike (105): All of a company's employees participate in the strike — 162

Industry strike (106): All the workers in a locality and given industry participate in the strike — 163

Sympathetic strike (107): Unions that are uninvolved in an issue also strike in solidarity with others — 164

RESTRICTED STRIKES

Detailed strike (108): Organized strike in which an increasing number of laborers stop working over a set time period — 165

Bumper strike (109): Unions strike one firm at a time — 166

Slowdown strike (110): Working slowly and inefficiently to undermine the employer — 167

Working-to-rule strike (111): Meticulously following all rules and regulations of a job without putting in any extra effort in order to slow down efficiency — 168

"Reporting 'sick' (sick-in)" (112): Large number of workers falsely claim to be ill — 169

Strike by resignation (113): En masse resignation by personnel — 170

Limited strike (114): Workers refuse certain amounts of work—overtime or certain days — 171

Selective strike (115): Workers refuse to perform certain tasks, usually due to moral or political qualms — 172

MULTI-INDUSTRY STRIKES

Generalized strike (116): Strike carried out in several industries at once, but not by a majority of workers — 173

General strike (117): Strike carried out by workers of various professions and industries in a region in order to bring it to an economic standstill — 174

COMBINATION OF STRIKES & ECONOMIC CLOSURES

Hartal (118): Voluntarily abstaining from economic activity for a set amount of time as a symbolic gesture   175

Economic shutdown (119): General strike and merchants' general strike   176

Political Noncooperation

REJECTION OF AUTHORITY

Withholding or withdrawal of allegiance (120): Refusal to recognize the validity of an authority or follow its orders   177

Refusal of public support (121): Public withholds support requested or demanded by a leader or public figure   178

Literature and speeches advocating resistance (122): Text that denounces an authority and promotes defiance   179

CITIZENS' NONCOOPERATION WITH GOVERNMENT

Boycott of legislative bodies (123): Refusal to serve in legislative branches of government   180

Boycott of elections (124): Refusal to participate in an election—frequently by an opposition faction   181

Boycott of government employment and positions (125): Refusal to fulfill the obligations of a government post   182

Boycott of government depts., agencies, and other bodies (126): Refusal to interact with or cooperate with a government agency or similar organization   183

Withdrawal from government educational institutions (127): Mass removal of one's children from public or government-run schools   184

Boycott of government-supported organizations (128): Refusal to interact with or cooperate with organizations which collaborate with the government   185

Refusal of assistance to enforcement agents (129): Refusal to supply police, military, or similar enforcement mechanisms with information or aid   186

Removal of own signs and placemarks (130): Removal or alteration of signs that assist with direction in order to misdirect or impede authorities   187

Refusal to accept appointed officials (131): Refusal to recognize authority of an official and responding with noncooperation when they attempt to fulfill their duties   188

Refusal to dissolve existing institutions (132): Refusal to accept government orders to dissolve an organization or institution   189

CITIZENS' ALTERNATIVES TO OBEDIENCE

Reluctant and slow compliance (133): Obedience that is carried out reluctantly or slowly in order to impede the process　190

Nonobedience in absence of direct supervision (134): Disobeying when no authority or command figure is present　191

Popular nonobedience (135): Widespread refusal to follow laws and regulations in a way that is not open or confrontational　192

Disguised disobedience (136): Action that appears to be compliant, but is in fact subversive in some way　193

Refusal of an assemblage or meeting to disperse (137): Continuing to gather after being told by an authority to leave　194

Sit-down (138): Sitting down and refusing to leave a space　195

Noncooperation with conscription and deportation (139): Form of conscientious objection—refusal to register or appear for conscription or to accede to deportation　196

Hiding, escape, and false identities (140): Fleeing or hiding one's identity to escape persecution or to protest a government policy　197

ACTION BY GOVERNMENT PERSONNEL

Legislative obstruction: Members of the lawmaking branch of government refusing to participate in a legislative process as an act of protest (i.e., delaying a quorum)　122

Selective refusal of assistance by government aides (142): Refusal by government employees to carry out certain orders　198

Blocking of lines of command and information (143): Deliberate interference in the chain of command and communication　199

Stalling and obstruction (144): Subtly working inefficiently to slow government action　200

General administrative noncooperation (145): Refusal to cooperate with a regime, usually one that has just come into power by illegitimate means, by the majority of government employees　201

Judicial noncooperation (146): Judges, jurors, and other judicial agents refuse to carry out their orders　202

Deliberate inefficiency and selective noncooperation by enforcement agents (147): Limited disobedience by police or similar enforcement agents　203

Mutiny (148): Open and outright disobedience by enforcement agents　204

Inter-agency noncooperation: Stopping support for other departments/ministries/agencies　205

DOMESTIC GOVERNMENTAL ACTION

Quasi-legal evasions and delays (149): Enacting laws that obstruct orders from a higher level of government, but does not directly contradict them   206

Noncooperation by constituent governmental units (150): Local governmental entities defying central authorities   207

INTERNATIONAL GOVERNMENTAL ACTION

Changes in diplomatic and other representations (151): Altering diplomatic staff/structures to show disapproval of a foreign government's policies or actions   208

Delay and cancellation of diplomatic events (152): Cancelling planned events to show disapproval of a foreign government   209

Withholding of diplomatic recognition (153): Refusing to recognize the legitimacy of a country's government   210

Severance of diplomatic relations (154): Terminating the relationship with another nation   211

Withdrawal from international organizations (155): Leaving an international group   212

Refusal of membership to international bodies (156): Refusing an invitation to join an international group   213

Expulsion from international organizations (157): Expelling a government from an interstate organization   214

Refraining: Positive Acts
(HOW ONE DOESN'T DO SOMETHING)

Suspension: Protesters temporarily cease an action, which is typically done in order to reward the opponent   215

Halting: Protesters terminate an action, which is typically done to reward the opponent   216

Active abstention from a planned action: Not going through with a threatened action, typically done to reward opponents for an action   217

Acts of Commission

(HOW ONE DOES SOMETHING)

Disruptive Commission

PSYCHOLOGICAL INTERVENTION

Protest disrobings (22): Removal of clothing in public as an expression of religious and/or political dissent 30

Protest sex: Engaging in public sexual activity as protest 37

Self-exposure to the elements (158): Exposing oneself to harsh environmental conditions (cold, heat, etc.) in order to pressure opponents into complying with requests 218

Fast of moral pressure (159a): Fasting to exert moral burdens on opponent 219

Hunger strike (159b): Fasting with intent of coercion 220

Satyagrahic fast (159c): Fast preceded by spiritual preparation with the intent to convert the opponent 221

Nonviolent harassment (161): Heightening pressures and agitations against perceived wrong doers 222

Self-mutilation (or body art) : Harming one's body as an act of protest/appeal; a highly controversial method of nonviolent action 223

Distributed Denial of Service (DDoS): Overloading a website by sending too many requests for access 225

Relay hunger strike: Strike in which participants take turns fasting in order to elongate the duration of the fast 300

PHYSICAL INTERVENTION

Gluing: Preventing public transport from running or blocking entry to buildings by super-gluing oneself to objects 79

Sit-in (162): Sitting in at a space in order to obstruct further access to the space, which typically will disturb routine activity 226

Nonviolent communication jamming: Hindering opponents' ability to use technological communication devices 227

Tripods: A large three-legged blockade device that resembles a camera tripod 228

Die-in: Pretending to die in a public space en masse; often used to signify the consequences of an opponents' destructive policies, beliefs, or actions 229

Book blocs: Participants of a human blockade use book-shaped constructed items as a type of shield and/or to spread a message 230

Boat blockade: Using boats to block other boats/entrances 231

Mill-in (166): Campaigners gather but remain mobile as they do so 232

Tree-sits: Barricading oneself to a public tree 233

Throwing food (pie-in): Using food as a nonviolent weapon 234

Destruction of public property: Destruction of public property; a highly controversial method of nonviolent action 235

Nonviolent air raids (169): Using nonviolent air transportation devices to drop significant items or pamphlets 236

Blocking demonstration: Using bodies and other items to impede the view of another demonstration 237

Nonviolent interjection (171): Physical intercession of someone's path, blocking their ability to execute their task in an attempt to make them reconsider (i.e., bulldozers or soldiers) 238

Nonviolent obstruction (172): Physical blocking of a space, creating a big enough obstacle to actually prevent passage 239

Inflatables: Use of inflatable items to obstruct, impede, and/or add an interactive element to a protest 240

Internal accompaniment: A person, potentially privileged, going with someone in a place that they might be at risk of harm 259

Chaining self/other: Using handcuffs, chains, bike locks, etc. to fasten an individual to an object/person that is significant to the protest 325

Destruction of government documents: Purposefully destroying government issued documents as a form of protest 327

Destruction of direct government objects: The destruction or damaging of government property to prevent direct violence 328

Covering public property/art: The act of erasing or covering opposing messages or symbols to prevent the public from continuing to see/experience them 329

Motor vehicle blockade: Using trucks, tractors, taxis, and cars to block traffic 330

Rebel clowning: Incorporating the practice of clowning into forms of organizing and protest/political disobedience 331

Suspending from bridges: Hanging from the side of a bridge, usually using ropes 332

Protest camp: Physical camps that are set up to delay, obstruct or prevent the focus of an opponent's protest by physically blocking it with the camp. 333

Solidarity accompaniment: A third-party's physical presence reduces the chance of violence toward a vulnerable community/individual 334

Preventing flights or public transportation from leaving: Preventing planes, or other forms of transportation from departing 335

SOCIAL INTERVENTION

Overloading of facilities (175): Deliberately overloading the capacity of a building or process so that operations efficiency is slowed down or stopped — 241

Stall-in (176): Customers/clients taking longer than normal to do something in order to slow down efficiency — 242

Speak-in (177): Campaigners interrupt gathering or event to raise an issue and speak for a prolonged period of time — 243

Public filibuster: Similar to a senatorial filibuster—an elongated speech intended to delay some aspect of a legislative process—but within the public realm — 244

Infiltration: Covertly sneaking into the opponent's gathering/event — 245

Guerrilla theater (178): Disruptive form of theater in which activists put on a surprise public performance that is designed to shock the audience — 246

Electoral guerrilla theater: Form of guerrilla theater in which someone runs for office as satirical social commentary — 247

Forum theater: Theater that addresses an issue but invites the audience at various points to participate and modify the performance — 248

Image theater: Like forum theater but participants stand still as if they are an image captured in reality — 249

Détournment/subvertising: Modifying a widely-known piece of art and giving it a new meaning that aligns with the activist's message — 250

Spreading rumors: Spreading unverified information in order to elicit a public response — 251

Hoax: Writing and spreading a false news story that is intended to be believed by the public — 252

Identity correction: Theatrically and publicly exposing an opponent's true, typically malicious, intentions/beliefs — 253

Invisible theater: Theater that does not seek to be recognized as such; public performance presented as reality — 254

Legislative theater: Form of political theater that asks the audience for suggestions of potential policy or legislative solutions to the problem presented in the performance — 255

Media-jacking: Subverting your opponent's media event/platform to benefit your own cause — 256

Creative disruption: Disrupting an event or talk in a unique way — 257

Alternative communication system (180): Using media to act outside of mainstream or monopolized communication (i.e., underground radio) — 258

Protective presence: A group placing itself in a position to deter the risk of harm to someone — 260

Third party witness: Acting as a non-involved third party by observing and potentially reporting on certain events — 261

Shouting down: Making it difficult for someone to speak by using a consistently higher volume — 336

ECONOMIC INTERVENTION

Reverse strike (181): Protesters or workers work harder than usual or continue to work when they are not supposed to   263

Stay-in strike (182): Workers stop working and refuse to leave a workspace until employers agree with requests   264

Politically motivated counterfeiting (185): Distributing counterfeit money to upset the economy   265

Preclusive purchasing (186): Deliberately buying certain commodities to prevent the opponent from having access to them   266

Seizure of assets (187): Impeding/confiscating the opponent's access to bank accounts, interest payments, copyrights/patents, or similar assets   267

Dumping (188): Selling a commodity at lower-than-market price to pressure a rival or opponent   268

Business whistleblowing: Individuals publicly expose illegal and/or immoral practices of banks, businesses, corporations, etc.   337

Land auction disruption: Preventing the sale of land from taking place   338

POLITICAL INTERVENTION

Whistleblowing — social, economic, political (outing): Leaking or alerting the public to information that is incriminating or elicits negative publicity   269

Overloading of administrative systems (193): Providing an excessive amount of information (which may or may not be relevant) to administrative systems in order to reduce progress and efficiency; can now be done digitally (for example, DDOS attacks)   270

Disclosing identities of secret agents (194): Publicly exposing the identity of a secret agent, which makes it difficult for them to continue their mission   271

Seeking imprisonment (195): Willful attempt to be arrested and jailed   272

Civil disobedience of "neutral" laws (196): Deliberate, open, and peaceful violation of "morally neutral" laws, decrees and regulations; acceptance of punishment   273

Work-on without collaboration (197): Protesters choosing to continue behaviors from a previous administration/hierarchy   274

Guerrilla legal work: Secretly building a legal case, typically through covert means   275

Parliamentary/legislature/council disruption: Stopping or slowing down legislative proceedings by extra-legal or extra-regulatory means; disruption often happens through shouting, singing, chanting   339

Absurd political candidates/parties: Creating outlandish or satiric political opponents to distract the main candidates or pull them towards a more centrist viewpoint   340

Creative Intervention/Prefigurative Actions
(HOW ONE MAKES OR CREATES SOMETHING)

POLITICAL & LEGAL ACTIONS

Mock elections (17): A purely symbolic election, either public or private, designed to educate or protest — 276

Social disobedience (63): Defiance of social norms, which is modeled after civil disobedience but without the legal violation — 277

Dual sovereignty and parallel government (198): Creating a new government with its own political institutions and organizational structures — 278

Civil disobedience of "illegitimate" laws (141): Open violation of unjust laws — 279

Reverse trial (160): Courtroom trials in which the accused—through words and body language—assumes the role of prosecutor, putting on trial the law or policy in question — 280

Citizen inspection: Illegal searches and seizures performed by private citizens — 341

ECONOMIC ACTIONS

Black markets: Secret trading areas, often selling illegal goods — 107

Refusal of a government's money (91): Refusing a particular currency — 281

Alternative markets (190): Creating alternative, illegal channels for buying and selling goods and services — 282

Alternative economic institutions (192): Creating new economic institutions (i.e., consumers' or producers' cooperatives) that are used to exert power/influence — 283

Copyleft/distributing copyrighted materials: Ignoring copyright laws and posting or distributing protected texts/materials — 284

Nonviolent land seizure (183): Nonviolent occupations in which the campaigners expect that the ownership of the land or facility will shift to them when they win the struggle — 285

Selective patronage "buycotts" (189): Activists promote and reward businesses who comply with the core principles of the campaign — 286

Conditional favorable loans: Activists provide loans to businesses, under the agreement that the business will promote practices and ideas that comply with the activists' cause — 303

Reverse pay-per-view: Providing money in exchange for views (of a documentary, short video, etc.) — 305

Property expropriation: Protesters seize abandoned or bankrupt private property to use for their cause — 342

Patent alternatives: Violating patent laws for positive reasons (e.g., life-saving medication) — 343

Socially responsible standards: A set of principles and benchmarks for corporations developed by civil society; enforced through buycotts, boycotts, legislation, and shareholder resolutions — 344

PHYSICAL ACTIONS

Tree planting: Planting trees in areas where it is prohibited to do so or where they would not otherwise be planted   60

Liberated zones: Claiming and blocking off a street or other public domain for performances or other movements   262

Nonviolent invasion (170): Entering an off-limits area to protest against government control of the land in question   288

Nonviolent occupation (173): Continuing to remain in an area after a nonviolent invasion   289

Stand-in (163): Continuing to stand and obstruct activity in a place where one is being refused service or entrance   290

Ride-in (164): Disobeying enforced segregation on public transport; most famously used by "freedom riders" during the US Civil Rights Movement   291

Wade-in (165): Those who are excluded from a public water space enter it anyways; widely used to combat segregation   292

Nonviolent raids (168): Protestors march to an area and declare rightful ownership   296

Defiance of blockades (184): Refusal to obey international blockades and providing food or other supplies to a blockaded place.   297

Kiss-in: Using public displays of physical affection as protest   299

Critical mass (cycling): Mass protests by cyclists reclaiming the streets from motor vehicles   345

SOCIAL ACTIONS

Symbolic reclamations (29): Creative use or claiming of appropriated things or symbols (cultivating a garden on public land, etc.)   39

Establishing new social patterns (174): The creation of new social institutions, planned and unplanned   287

Pray-in (167): Praying in a public or private space in an obstructive manner, including in churches   293

New signs and names (27): Revising/removing street signs or installing new ones   294

Alternative transportation systems (191): Creating an alternative transportation system in addition to boycotting the pre-existing one   295

Women becoming religious leaders without official approval: Women assuming leadership in the Church without being expressly allowed to do so   301

Distributing free VPNs and alternative apps: Distributing internet tools that allow people to evade government censors or ISP monitoring   302

Living memorial: Memorials that continue to grow or that honor those who are still living   318

Marriage inclusion: Marriages performed without state approval (for example, same-sex, cross-religion, cross-caste, interracial, etc.)   326

PSYCHOLOGICAL ACTIONS

Self-imposed transparency: Deliberate organizational transparency about ongoing affairs and issues 298

Flowers in guns: Placing a flower into the mouth of a gun to symbolize the need for peace over violence 304

Awards as encouragement: Giving awards to those who tentatively align with the movement's goals to encourage their actions 306

For further updates, check the Nonviolent Tactics Database available at **tactics.nonviolenceinternational.net**

For inquiries and suggestions for new tactics/methods or forms of nonviolent action and civil resistance, please send emails to **info@nonviolenceinternational.net**

Acknowledgements

We are indebted to Gene Sharp for his lifetime of contributions to the field of nonviolent action and his collection and classification of nonviolent methods upon which we build. He blessed my efforts to expand his collection of nonviolent tactics and write this monograph.

I want to thank those who inspired me early in my career including Charlie Walker, Bob Helvey, Sulak Sivaraksa, George Willoughby, Lynne Shivers, George Lakey, and Bill Moyer.

The work of collecting and cataloguing tactics from all over the world has been the collective effort of many interns and volunteers at Nonviolence International.

That list includes Nicholas Anders, Seth Barry-Hinton, India Zietsman, Lara al Qasem, Matt Barr, Netty Brinckerhoff, Nick Shedd, Kimmy Baagelaar, Kimberle Maro, Sarah Bausmith, Michael Konen, Nicholas Scrimenti, Sarah Knorr, Rachel Lewis, Daniel Jarrad, Liam Glen, Ryan Flynn, Shelby Rogers, Emily Hill, Jilian Maulella, Emily Mattioli, Pjotr Tabachnikoff, Annalisa Bell, Connor Paul, Alyssa Scott, and Tiffany Schwartz.

This monograph has taken three years to formulate and write. Those who have provided their time and advice include Nadine Bloch, Kurt Schock, Véronique Dudouet, Stephen Zunes and Doug Bond.

I want to thank the editors Maciej Bartkowski, Steve Chase, Amber French, and Julia Constantine and the entire enterprise at the International Center on Nonviolent Conflict (ICNC) led by Hardy Merriman and Peter Ackerman. ICNC's contribution to the field of civil resistance continues to be enormous and I hope it will do so for many decades to come.

I want to thank Mubarak Awad, Jonathan Kuttab, Betty Sitka, Paul Magno, and David Hart who have served on the staff or board of Nonviolence International and who have tolerated and supported me for so many years.

Finally, I want to thank my family, especially my loving parents, John and Fran Beer who so profoundly shaped my interests and values, my siblings Jenny and Matthew, who have provided advice, more of which I wish I had followed. My spouse Latanja and kids, Kian and Skye, are such blessings in my life and they have been so patient and understanding. This monograph and the Nonviolent Tactics Database would not exist without them.

About the Author

Michael A. Beer serves as the Director of Nonviolence International, an innovative and respected Washington, DC based nonprofit promoting nonviolent approaches to international conflicts. Since 1991 he has worked with NVI to serve marginalized people who seek to use nonviolent tactics often in difficult and dangerous environments. This includes diaspora activists, multinational coalitions, global social movements, as well as within countries including: Myanmar, Tibet, Indonesia, Russia, Thailand, Palestine, Cambodia, East Timor, Iran, India, Kosovo, Zimbabwe, Sudan, and the United States. Michael Beer has a special expertise in supporting movements against dictators and in support of global organizing for justice, environment, and peace. Michael co-parents two teenagers with his patient life partner, Latanja.

A Note from the Author

The power of nonviolent social change is immense and is shaping the world every single day. There is not a minute that goes by where there is not a street protest, hunger strike, blockade, boycott or work stoppage happening somewhere in the world. I have been studying and collecting nonviolent tactics, examples, and photos for more than 30 years and have only scratched the surface of the large range of activities that people are engaging in to change the world.

I invite you to contribute to the ongoing collection and classification of nonviolent tactics on the website: **https://tactics.nonviolenceinternational.net**. You can find a form on the website where I urge you to share your input. We also welcome editors willing to help manage the website and its content.

If you would like to have me or my Nonviolence International colleagues such as Mubarak Awad speak to your class or group about the book and the vast creative universe of nonviolent tactics, please contact me at **info@nonviolenceinternational.net**.

I hope you enjoy the book and I look forward to being in conversation with you.

Sincerely,

Michael A. Beer
Director, Nonviolence International